THERE'S NOTHING LIKE IT!

THERE'S NOTHING LIKE IT!

A Devotional Journey Through the Great Commandment

Advantage
BOOKS

Dr. John R. Adolph

Library of Congress Catalog Number: APPLIED FOR	
Name:	Adolph, John R., Author
Title:	*There's Nothing Like It: A Devotional Journey Through the Great Commandment* John R. Adolph Advantage Books, 2025
Identifiers:	ISBN Paperback: 9781597558754 ISBN eBook: 9781597558860
Subjects:	Books › Religion & Spirituality › Worship & Devotion Devotionals Books › Religion & Spirituality › Worship & Devotion Inspirational Books › Religion & Spirituality › Worship & Devotion Prayer

First Printing: January 2026
26 27 28 29 30 31 32   10 9 8 7 6 5 4 3 2 1

Table of Contents

ACKNOWLEDGMENTS

✦ ✦ ✦

Now Unto Him!

Every word, in these pages, is an echo of Your grace. Thank You for loving me first, calling me to preach the Gospel, and trusting me to shepherd Your people. Your love is the source, the substance, and the signature of this work. In short, love wins because You do. I bow before You and will forever worship You and You alone!

To my family.

To my beautiful wife and faithful partner in life and ministry: thank you for your love, patience, and unshakable support when the days were long and the deadlines were close. To my children: thank you for cheering me on, praying me through, and reminding me to laugh. You are living proof that God's love still writes the best stories. I love you!

To the Antioch Missionary Baptist Church family (Beaumont, Texas).

You are an answered prayer. Thank you for letting me serve you, learn with you, and love you. Your hunger for the Word and your heart for people inspired every paragraph. This devotional carries your fingerprints, your testimonies, your tears, and your triumphs. Antioch, I appreciate you!

To our leadership teams.

To the Executive Staff and Executive Church Officers, our Deacons and Deaconesses, to the Associate Ministers and Ministers' Spouses, Trustees, and the entire staff, thank you for excellence behind the scenes and faithfulness in the trenches. To our Intercessory Prayer Team, your knees made this possible. To our Worship and Arts, Media/Audio Visual, and Creative Teams, thank you for giving this message voice, sound, and sight. To our Ministry Coordinators and Ministry Leaders, thank you for turning truths into transformation week after week. I'm indebted to you!

To the servant leaders and volunteers.

Greeters, ushers, ministry servants, outreach, children and youth workers, and every faithful volunteer, thank you for loving people where they are and helping them find their way to Jesus. You make love visible. I celebrate you!

To the editorial and design collaborators.

To every editor, proofreader, and publishing partner who helped shape and polish these pages, thank you so very much for helping me make sure that this book is excellent. To the layout and cover designer who clothed this word in beauty, thank you for your awesome work that shows the world what the Gospel looks like. I cherish you!

To mentors, colleagues, cohorts and friends in ministry.

Thank you for modeling integrity, generosity, and courage. Your counsel and encouragement strengthened my hands and settled my heart. I honor you!

To my institutions of higher academic achievement and my instructors.

With gratitude to the Morehouse School of Religion (ITC, MDiv), the Houston Graduate School of Theology (DMin) and Grace School of Theology (Adjunct), thank you for equipping my mind and igniting my mission. To every professor and classmate, who sharpened me, please know that your investment continues to bear fruit. I bless you!

To our extended Antioch family online.

For every worshipper, partner, and friend who joined us through broadcasts and digital ministry, thank you for leaning in, sharing, giving, participating and praying. God used your online presence to push this work across the finish line. I will never forget you!

Special thanks.

To all of you who took the time to simply encourage me along the way. Where names are many and memory is finite, please receive this as a heartfelt embrace from your Pastor. I highly regard you!

Scripture notice.

All Scripture quotations are taken from the King James Version (KJV) and are in the public domain.

Better Together and Higher Than The Top,

Dr. John R. Adolph, Pastor

"And now abideth faith, hope, love, these three; but the greatest of these is love." (1 Corinthians 13:13, KJV)

Dr. John R. Adolph

INTRODUCTION

Core Value 2 | The Great Commandment: There's Nothing Like It!

At Antioch Missionary Baptist Church, we are a congregation built on the Word of God and grounded in three Core Values that define who we are and why we exist. These Core Values are not slogans or statements, they are our spiritual DNA. They are the foundation beneath our faith, the principles that shape our purpose, and the compass that directs our mission in the world.

Core Value 1 reminds us that we are co-missionaries with the person of Jesus Christ. We are in the Kingdom business of going, teaching and baptizing as the Great Commission commands us to do.

Core Value 2, the purpose of this book, compels us to live out the Great Commandment of Jesus Christ: to love God with all our heart, soul, and mind, and to love our neighbor as ourselves.

Core Value 3 reminds us to fulfill the Great Calling, to become fishers of men, winning the souls of fallen humanity through the amazing grace God provided for us at the cross of Jesus Christ.

These three values form the heartbeat of Antioch. Right at the center of that heartbeat is love; the pure, powerful, redemptive love of Jesus Christ that flows from the Father through the Holy Spirit, to us for the purpose of reaching the world with the message of the Gospel.

This book, THERE'S NOTHING LIKE IT!, is an invitation to walk deeper into that love. It is more than a devotional, it is a spiritual journey. Every page will cause you to reflect, to grow, to forgive, to serve, and to love more intentionally than ever before. This book presents Core Value 2, The Great Commandment of Jesus Christ, to those who are ready to faithfully obey Him by sharing His light of love with the world.

This devotional series focuses on our expressions of love towards self and those facets of love that strengthen our relationship with God and with others. Section One, "There's Nothing Like Loving Me," teaches us the importance of healthy, God-centered self-love, the kind that begins in grace, not arrogance. Section Two, "There's Nothing Like Loving You," moves outward, showing us how to love people the way Jesus loves them: real, raw, and redemptive. Section Three, "There's Nothing Like Loving God," calls us upward, helping us rediscover the wonder of worship and the beauty of full devotion. Section Four, "There's Nothing Like God Loving Me," brings the journey full circle, reminding us that all love starts with Him. It's the revelation that fuels the relationship.

Each chapter flows with divine intentionality. Within these pages, you'll find a group assignment that starts the week along with six daily devotionals written to help you meditate on Scripture, apply truth to daily life, and build spiritual strength through prayer and reflection. Every devotional follows a pattern designed for transformation:

- "Straight from the Book" grounds you in the Word of God.

- "Jesus Said It Best" reveals how Christ's teaching connects to the theme.

- "Pastor Puts It Like This" translates the truth into practical, everyday application with pastoral insight and humor.

- "Think About It for a Moment" challenges your heart with reflection and self-examination.

- "Pray About It" draws you into intimate conversation with God, ending every reflection with the same declaration of faith: In the Name of Jesus, Amen!

If you want to maximize your spiritual growth as you read this book, don't rush it. Take time each day to sit with the Scripture. Read it out loud. Let the Spirit highlight what He's saying to you personally. Write down what stands out. Share what you're learning with someone else. Then put love into practice because revelation without action is just information.

This devotional isn't meant to stay on your shelf. It's meant to stay in your spirit. Every day's reflection is a seed, and if you water it with faith and obedience, it will bear the fruit of transformation.

You are about to encounter truth that heals, restores, and challenges. You are about to experience the love of God in ways that reach beyond emotions into every area of your life. You are about to walk through the Word and God's Word changes everything for the greater.

So, turn the page with expectation! Open your heart with anticipation. Let this be more than a devotional reading, let it be a revival!

Because at Antioch, and in the Kingdom of God, LOVE WINS!

Dr. John R. Adolph

SECTION I - *Week One*

THERE'S NOTHING LIKE LOVING ME!

Scripture Lesson: St. Matthew 22:39

Today's Subject: LOVING ME AND LOVING IT!

KEY POINTS FROM TODAY'S LESSON

Point 1

_____

_____

_____

_____

_____

Point 2

_____

_____

_____

_____

_____

Point 3

_____

_____

_____

_____

_____

Here's What I'm Praying For Right Now:

_____

_____

_____

_____

_____

_____

_____

_____

_____

DAY 2: "Mirror Talk"

STRAIGHT FROM THE BOOK

"And the second is like unto it, Thou shalt love thy neighbour as thyself."
(Matthew 22:39, KJV)

JESUS SAID IT BEST

When Jesus said this, He revealed that love begins with reflection. The mirror of the soul shows how you truly see yourself. Many people avoid self-reflection because it reveals both beauty and brokenness. But Jesus' words invite us to see ourselves through God's mirror not the world's. His love defines your worth, not your mistakes or people's opinions. When you understand that, your reflection becomes revelation. You stop seeing your flaws and start seeing His favor.

PASTOR PUTS IT LIKE THIS

Some people avoid mirrors because they don't like what's looking back; not just physically, but spiritually. But let me share something life-changing with you, you can't fix what you won't face! You will never conquer anything that you refuse to confront. Look in that mirror today and tell yourself, "God made me on purpose, for a purpose." The mirror ain't your enemy; it's your ministry tool. Love who you see because that's the person God is using to change the world.

THINK ABOUT IT FOR A MOMENT

- What do you see when you look at yourself through God's eyes?
- "You can't heal what you chose to hide."
- True self-love starts with honest self-reflection.

PRAY ABOUT IT

Lord, help me to see myself the way You see me: redeemed, renewed, and radiant in Your image. Heal my self-image and restore my confidence in You.

In the name of Jesus, Amen!

DAY 3: "No More Self-Sabotage"

STRAIGHT FROM THE BOOK

"And the second is like unto it, Thou shalt love thy neighbour as thyself."
(Matthew 22:39, KJV)

JESUS SAID IT BEST

Loving yourself means refusing to partner with your own destruction. Jesus never taught self-pity or self-sabotage, He taught self-respect and discipline. Every time you doubt your value, you agree with the enemy's lie. Every time you talk yourself out of what God called you to do, you're sabotaging your own purpose. Jesus came to free us from self-defeat by showing us how to walk in divine identity.

PASTOR PUTS IT LIKE THIS

You can't keep saying, "I'm not enough" and expect to win! You can't keep saying "I'm kicking, but not high" and expect to come out on top. You can't keep saying "I can't" and expect to live a life of things done well. At some point, you have to stop killing yourself with negative views and satanic lies. Some of us have been our own worst enemy. The devil doesn't have to fight hard when we're beating ourselves up. Stop calling yourself "less than" when God calls you "chosen". You've got to quit digging graves for dreams that God's still breathing on. Speak life to yourself! That's self-love in action.

THINK ABOUT IT FOR A MOMENT

- What's one area of your life where you've been sabotaging your success?
- "Stop setting yourself on fire to keep others warm."
- Victory starts with agreement! Agree with God about who you are.

PRAY ABOUT IT

Lord, break the cycle of self-sabotage in my life. Teach me to walk in confidence, courage, and clarity. I believe what You say about me.

In the name of Jesus, Amen!

DAY 4: "Learning to Forgive Yourself"

STRAIGHT FROM THE BOOK

"And the second is like unto it, Thou shalt love thy neighbour as thyself." **(Matthew 22:39, KJV)**

JESUS SAID IT BEST

Jesus never condemned the broken; He restored them. He told the woman caught in sin, "Go and sin no more," not "Live in guilt forever." Loving yourself includes forgiving yourself. Grace isn't just something we extend to others; it's something we must receive ourselves. The cross wasn't just for your neighbor; it was for you too. Jesus never said "forgive yourself." However, He did say, ".... love thy neighbour as thyself." With this in mind, it is imperative to realize that you cannot have one without the other. To love is to forgive.

PASTOR PUTS IT LIKE THIS

You can't keep beating yourself up for what Jesus already paid for. You're carrying guilt that grace has already covered. Some of us keep reliving yesterday like we can rewrite it. You can't! But you can start a new page today. Forgive yourself for being flawed, and thank God for being faithful. When you let go of guilt, you make room for growth. When you get past your failures, you position your life for progress that is yet **(in the)** future. In short, get over it and move on!

THINK ABOUT IT FOR A MOMENT

- What would it look like to forgive yourself completely?
- "Don't trip over what's behind you."
- Grace means you can get up without guilt.

PRAY ABOUT IT

Lord, thank You for forgiving me when I couldn't forgive myself. Teach me to walk free from shame and full of grace. In the name of Jesus, Amen!

DAY 5: "Boundaries Are Holy"

STRAIGHT FROM THE BOOK

**"And the second is like unto it, Thou shalt love thy neighbour as thyself."
(Matthew 22:39, KJV)**

JESUS SAID IT BEST

Jesus loved everyone, but He didn't please everyone. He healed multitudes but still withdrew to pray. He set holy boundaries because He understood His purpose. Loving yourself means protecting your peace, your time, and your spirit. You can't save people you're called to serve if you're always running on empty. Boundaries are not selfish, they're sacred.

PASTOR PUTS IT LIKE THIS

Some people think "being nice" means saying "yes" to everything, this is not true! Even Jesus said "no" sometimes. You can't pour from an empty cup. Set some boundaries, and don't apologize for them. You're not being mean; you're being wise. Love yourself enough to rest, recharge, and say "no" when God says, "not now." Here's a great remedy a wise man once taught me pertaining to rest on the regular: one day a week rest, one week a month rest, and one month a year rest. God will honor it and you will discover that you needed it.

THINK ABOUT IT FOR A MOMENT

- What boundaries do I need to set for my mental and spiritual health?
- "No" is a holy word when it protects your peace.
- Peace is proof that you're prioritizing God's order.

PRAY ABOUT IT

Lord, give me the wisdom to set healthy boundaries and the courage to keep them. Help me guard my peace and protect my purpose.

In the name of Jesus, Amen!

DAY 6: "You're Worth It"

STRAIGHT FROM THE BOOK

"And the second is like unto it, Thou shalt love thy neighbour as thyself."
(Matthew 22:39, KJV)

JESUS SAID IT BEST

Jesus left Heaven for you. He gave up the golden streets of glory for the dusty streets of Galilee for you. He gave up the praises of angels for the curses of men for you. He became sin for you. He became a prisoner so that you could go free. He gave up Heaven and went to hell, so that you could miss going to hell and live eternally with Him in Heaven! He thought you were worth the nails, worth the cross, worth the resurrection. That means your worth isn't up for debate. Self-love rooted in Christ means understanding your value in God's eyes. You are worth loving, worth healing, worth growing. Jesus didn't die for discounts, He died for destiny. He didn't pay half price. He paid the full price!

PASTOR PUTS IT LIKE THIS

Stop acting like you're on the clearance sale rack when God says you're couture! You're not a mistake; you're a masterpiece. Walk like it. Talk like it. Treat yourself like someone Jesus died for because He did! Don't let people who don't know your value put a price tag on your worth. When God made you, He broke the mold.

THINK ABOUT IT FOR A MOMENT

- Do I see myself as valuable to God?
- "You are fearfully and wonderfully made and not cheaply and carelessly assembled."
- Self-worth is not arrogance; it's awareness.

PRAY ABOUT IT

Lord, thank You for reminding me that I'm worth loving and worth saving. Help me live like someone You died for.

In the name of Jesus, Amen!

DAY 7: "I'm Still Becoming"

STRAIGHT FROM THE BOOK

> **"And the second is like unto it, Thou shalt love thy neighbour as thyself."**
> **(Matthew 22:39, KJV)**

JESUS SAID IT BEST

Jesus often spoke about growth. His lessons often talked about seeds, vines, and branches because love is a process. You don't become confident overnight. You grow in grace. Loving yourself includes patience with your process. God is still shaping you, developing you, and maturing your faith. Jesus doesn't demand perfection; He desires **progress. This** is evident because He did not fire any of His disciples who never got it right. He was patient with them. He forgave them. He worked with them and on them at the same time. He loved them.

PASTOR PUTS IT LIKE THIS

You're a work in progress, not a piece of junk! Don't rush the recipe God's cooking up in your life. The best dishes take time, and likewise, so does destiny. Stop comparing your chapter two to somebody's chapter twenty. God's still working on you, and that's a good thing. Celebrate your growth and trust the process.

THINK ABOUT IT FOR A MOMENT

- Where can I celebrate progress instead of perfection?
- "Be patient with yourself, God's not done yet."
- You are becoming who God already saw.

PRAY ABOUT IT

Lord, thank You for not giving up on me. Help me to love myself while You finish what You started in me.

In the name of Jesus, Amen!

CONCLUSION | Week One | "I LOVE ME"

As We Conclude Week One…

This week we have learned that LOVE WINS! This study has centered on the truth Jesus teaches in Matthew 22:36–40, reminding us that loving God, loving others, and loving ourselves are inseparably connected.

Below is a biblical summation of what students should now understand after studying together.

WHAT WE LEARNED THIS WEEK

1. Self-Love Is Built Into the Greatest Commandments

Scripture: Matthew 22:37–39

Jesus says the second commandment is to "love thy neighbour as thyself."

Biblically, self-love is a requirement, not a suggestion.

Without loving yourself, you cannot fulfill either the commandment to love God rightly (Deut. 6:5) or to love others sacrificially (John 13:34–35).

2. You Cannot Pour From an Empty Cup

Scripture:

- Proverbs 4:23 | "Keep thy heart with all diligence…"
- Mark 1:35 | Jesus withdrew to pray and rest.
- Psalm 23:3 | "He restoreth my soul."

Jesus modeled spiritual, emotional, and physical replenishment.

His pattern teaches us that caring for ourselves positions us to care for others.

3. Christ-Centered Self-Love Is Not Ego, It Is Identity

Scripture:

- Psalm 139:14 | "I am fearfully and wonderfully made."
- Ephesians 2:10 | "We are His workmanship…"
- Genesis 1:27 | Made in God's image.

Self-love is not pride; it is accepting God's truth about how He created you. Your worth is not determined by people, it is determined by God Himself (Romans 8:31–39).

4. Many Believers Treat Others Better Than They Treat Themselves

Scripture:

- Romans 8:1 | "There is therefore now no condemnation…"
- Psalm 34:5 | "They looked unto Him and were lightened…"
- 1 John 3:20 | God is greater than our self-condemnation.

We learned that God does not call us to harshness toward ourselves, He calls us to grace, mercy, and renewal. The enemy thrives where shame lives, but God calls us to freedom.

5. Loving Yourself Is Stewardship of God's Property

Scripture:

- 1 Corinthians 6:19–20 | "You are not your own… glorify God in your body."
- Matthew 25:14–30 | Stewardship matters.
- John 10:10 | Jesus came that we "might have life… abundantly."

You belong to God. Taking care of your emotional, physical, and spiritual health honors Him. Self-love equals stewardship. You care for yourself because God created you, redeemed you, and indwells you.

6. The Voice You Speak to Yourself With Must Agree With God

Scripture:

- Proverbs 18:21 | "Life and death are in the power of the tongue."
- Philippians 4:8 | Think on truth, virtue, and praise.
- Joel 3:10 | "Let the weak say, 'I am strong".

You learned this week that your self-talk must match what God has spoken: Loved. Chosen. Valued. Forgiven. Redeemed!

Any voice contrary to God's voice must be rejected.

7. Loving Yourself Is Not Vanity, It's Victory

Scripture:

- Romans 12:3 | Sobriety of self-view: neither too high nor too low.

- Galatians 5:13–14 | Love fulfills the law.
- Song of Solomon 4:7 | "You are altogether beautiful…"

Self-love strengthens discipleship, relationships, purpose, and emotional resilience. It lifts you from comparison (Gal. 6:4) and roots you in God's love (Jer. 31:3).

WEEK *One* TAKEAWAYS

By the end of Week One, believers should confidently affirm:

- "God commands me to love myself." (Matthew 22:39)
- "My identity is rooted in God's creation." (Genesis 1:27)
- "I reject shame and condemnation." (Romans 8:1)
- "I am God's masterpiece." (Ephesians 2:10)
- "Loving myself honors God." (1 Corinthians 6:19–20)

This week was not about inflating the ego, but it was about aligning identity with God's Word.

WEEK *One* FINAL PRAYER

Lord, thank You for the revelation You have given us this week. Thank You for teaching us that loving ourselves is not pride, sin, or selfishness, but it is obedience to Your Word (John 15:12). Heal every wound that destroys our self-worth. Uproot every lie that contradicts Your truth that remains in our lives. Restore the joy, confidence, and clarity You designed us to carry.

Teach us to see ourselves as fearfully and wonderfully made (Psalm 139:14). Teach us to steward our lives as Your workmanship (Ephesians 2:10). Teach us to walk in love toward You, ourselves, and others (Matthew 22:36–40).Let Your love flow to us, in us, and through us as we continue this journey of transformation.

In the name of Jesus, Amen.

SECTION I - *Week Two*

DAY 1: THE GROUP ENCOUNTER

THERE'S NOTHING LIKE LOVING ME!

Scripture Lesson: Genesis 1:27

Today's Subject: HAND CRAFTED BY THE FINEST!

KEY POINTS FROM TODAY'S LESSON

Point 1

_____

_____

_____

_____

_____

Point 2

_____

_____

_____

_____

_____

Point 3

_____

_____

_____

_____

_____

Here's What I'm Praying For Right Now:

_____

_____

_____

_____

_____

_____

_____

_____

_____

DAY 2: "Stamped by Heaven"

STRAIGHT FROM THE BOOK

"So God created man in his own image, in the image of God created he him; male and female created he them." (Genesis 1:27, KJV)

JESUS SAID IT BEST

Jesus said, "Render unto Caesar the things that are Caesar's, and unto God the things that are God's." Coins carried Caesar's image, and you are made to carry God's image. That means you belong to Him! His stamp on your life makes you valuable beyond measure. When life tries to devalue you, remember this: your worth comes from whose image you bear, not what season you're in.

PASTOR PUTS IT LIKE THIS

Ever notice how a one hundred bill doesn't lose value just because it's been crumpled? You can step on it, wrinkle it, even drop it in the mud, but it's still worth the same! That's you. You've been through stuff, but you're still stamped by Heaven. Your value doesn't decrease because of life's damage. You still belong to God, and He still plans to use you.

THINK ABOUT IT FOR A MOMENT
- What has tried to make me forget my value?
- "Life may bend you, but it can't break your worth."
- The image of God is permanent, not erasable.

PRAY ABOUT IT

Lord, thank You for the reminder that I am stamped with Your image. Let me never forget who I belong to.

In the name of Jesus, Amen!

DAY 3: "The Real Glow Up"

STRAIGHT FROM THE BOOK

> **"So God created man in his own image, in the image of God created he him; male and female created he them." (Genesis 1:27, KJV)**

JESUS SAID IT BEST

The world defines a "glow up" by looks, likes, and luxury. But Jesus defines transformation from the inside out. When your heart reflects His image, your whole life shines differently. You can't fake that kind of glow. It's the light of the Lord radiating through your spirit. Real confidence doesn't come from filters or followers; it comes from faith in the person of Jesus Christ, Son of the living God.

PASTOR PUTS IT LIKE THIS

Everybody loves a glow up! But let's be real, the best kind ain't cosmetic, it's Christmatic! When God lights you up, no one can dim your shine. You can wear designer clothes, but nothing looks better than peace. You can drive a nice car, but nothing rides smoother than grace. Let God do His makeover on your mind, and watch how your soul glows.

THINK ABOUT IT FOR A MOMENT

- What part of me needs a spiritual "glow up"?
- "Let your light so shine…" (Matthew 5:16)
- Beauty fades, but the image of God doesn't.

PRAY ABOUT IT

Lord, let Your light shine through me. Give me a glow that makeup can't match and filters can't fake.

In the name of Jesus, Amen!

DAY 4: "Built Different"

STRAIGHT FROM THE BOOK

> "So God created man in his own image, in the image of God created he him; male and female created he them." (Genesis 1:27, KJV)

JESUS SAID IT BEST

Jesus was both divine and human. He is fully God and completely human. This hypostatic union teaches us something powerful: we're made to live in two realms at once. You're physical, but you're also spiritual. You were built differently. When you understand that divine design, you stop settling for surface-level living. You were born with greatness wired into your soul because you reflect the greatness of your Creator. There is nothing mediocre or ordinary about you. Extraordinary! This is a great term that defines the totality of what God made when He engineered your very existence.

PASTOR PUTS IT LIKE THIS

When people say, "you're built different," take that as a compliment! God didn't make you average. You've got divine DNA running in your veins. That's why some people can't handle your energy, your effort, and your excellence. You carry Heaven's blueprint. Stop trying to blend in when you were built to stand out. Stop trying to copy other people when you were made to be an original. Let the God in you shine unapologetically.

THINK ABOUT IT FOR A MOMENT

- Am I living up to the divine design God put in me?
- "Normal is overrated; however, holy is powerful."
- You're not basic; you're blessed.

PRAY ABOUT IT

Lord, thank You for making me unique and extraordinary in Your image. Help me walk boldly in my divine design.

In the name of Jesus, Amen!

DAY 5: "Royal Bloodline"

STRAIGHT FROM THE BOOK

> "So God created man in his own image, in the image of God created he him; male and female created he them." (Genesis 1:27, KJV)

JESUS SAID IT BEST

Jesus called God "Our Father," introducing us to our spiritual heritage. Think about that for a moment. Okay, let's look at it from a different angle. Imagine that in creation, you had to come through an assembly line before you could be born, wired with everything that would be needed for you to be what God wanted you to be. Now imagine that your prototype is Jesus Christ! In other words, if God is King, that makes you royalty. You don't need a crown to be royal. You were born into a heavenly bloodline. Your identity in Christ gives you access to authority, favor, and inheritance. Loving yourself means remembering where you come from and who your Father is.

PASTOR PUTS IT LIKE THIS

You're not just from your mama's side or your daddy's side, you're from the side of the Most High! This should cause you to rejoice! Royalty runs in your blood. Stop acting like a peasant when you're the King's kid. Walk like it. Talk like it. Pray like it. And, have the audacity to live like it! You're covered in royal grace and you are wired with a heavenly swag.

THINK ABOUT IT FOR A MOMENT

- How does knowing I'm royal change how I see myself?
- "You can't walk in power while thinking in poverty."
- Remember who your Daddy is! He is the King of Kings!

PRAY ABOUT IT

Father, thank You for adopting me into Your royal family. Help me to walk with Kingdom confidence every day.

In the name of Jesus, Amen!

DAY 6: "Handle With Care"

STRAIGHT FROM THE BOOK

"So God created man in his own image, in the image of God created he him; male and female created he them." (Genesis 1:27, KJV)

JESUS SAID IT BEST

If you're made in God's image, that means you're sacred. Every part of you: body, soul, and spirit, deserves care and respect. Jesus valued the temple of the body and often rested, ate, and cared for Himself to keep His assignment strong. In this stead, Jesus took the time for self-care which reflected His love for Himself. Here's what we gain from observing the life of our Lord Jesus Christ, loving yourself means taking care of yourself: physically, mentally, emotionally, and spiritually. To love yourself is to love God's greatest possession on earth, you!

PASTOR PUTS IT LIKE THIS

Listen, you can't pray your way out of what rest will fix! Even Jesus took naps. You can't be everything for everybody. To be available is one thing, but to be convenient is another. Don't feel guilty for taking care of yourself. That's not weakness; that's wisdom. Treat yourself like a temple, not a trash can. Eat better, think better, live better because the God who lives in you deserves the best version of you possible.

THINK ABOUT IT FOR A MOMENT

- What's one way I can take better care of myself this week?
- "Self-care is soul-care."
- Rest is holy, not lazy.

PRAY ABOUT IT

Lord, help me to handle myself with care, as Your creation made in Your image. Teach me to protect my peace and nurture my temple.

In the name of Jesus, Amen!

DAY 7: "Two Peas in a Pod"

STRAIGHT FROM THE BOOK

"So God created man in his own image, in the image of God created he him; male and female created he them." (Genesis 1:27, KJV)

JESUS SAID IT BEST

When God created humanity, He made two: male and female, with equal dignity, equal beauty, and equal worth. The Father created no duplicates, but He did create compatibility. He designed us to reflect His image not in isolation, but in community, connection, and in healthy relational constructs that remind the world of who He is.

Jesus affirmed this unity when He taught about marriage, friendship, forgiveness, and love. He consistently showed that people were designed to walk together. In the kingdom, no one becomes their best self alone. Growth happens in kingdom partnerships, friendships and Christ-centered collaborations. In short, healing happens in community. Strength is found in unity.

PASTOR PUTS IT LIKE THIS

God didn't create you to go through life as a solo project, but He made you to connect. "Two peas in a pod" isn't just a cute phrase; it's a picture of God's design. Men and women weren't made to compete, compare, or tear each other down. They were made to complement each other and bring out the best in one another.

THINK ABOUT IT FOR A MOMENT

- How have I honored (or dishonored) the God-image in others?
- "Unity is God's design, division is the devil's distraction."

PRAY ABOUT IT

Lord, thank You for creating me in Your image and surrounding me with people who also reflect Your glory. Teach me to honor others as You honor them. Help me celebrate differences, walk in unity, and recognize Your presence in every person You've made.

In the name of Jesus, Amen!

CONCLUSION | Week Two| "IN HIS IMAGE: LOVING ME BECAUSE GOD MADE US!"
As We Conclude Week Two...

This week we centered our hearts and minds on Genesis 1:27:

"So God created man in His own image, in the image of God created He him; male and female created He them."

This study reminded us that self-love does not begin with self, it begins with God's design. We love ourselves correctly when we understand our identity biblically. The reason we honor ourselves is simple: **God made us!** God mirrored Himself in us.

Below is a biblical summation of what students should know after studying together.

WHAT WE LEARNED THIS WEEK
1. Loving Myself Begins With Knowing Who Made Me
Scripture: Genesis 1:27; Psalm 100:3

Self-love is not rooted in feelings or culture. It is rooted in creation. God Himself formed you, shaped you, breathed into you, and fashioned you on purpose. Loving yourself is agreeing with God's craftsmanship.

2. The Image of God Gives Every Person Inherent Worth
Scripture: Colossians 3:10; Psalm 8:4–5

Because we bear His image, we possess built-in dignity and divine value. You are not valuable because of what you do, but you are valuable because of who made you. With this in mind, self-love is not arrogance; it is acknowledgment that you are the handiwork of Almighty God.

3. I Cannot Love Myself If I Reject the Image of God in Me
Scripture: Ephesians 2:10; Isaiah 64:8

To hate yourself, belittle yourself, or condemn yourself is to insult the God who created you. You are not an accident, inconvenience, or mistake. You are God's intentional artistry. In this stead, self-love is worship when it honors the One who made you.

4. God Created Male and Female to Reflect His Nature Together

Scripture: Genesis 1:27; Genesis 2:18

Being created male and female shows God's desire for relationship and connection. Our differences do not diminish us, however, they display God's complexity and beauty. We love ourselves by celebrating our differences and sharing our similarities. Keep this in mind, God loves variety. In this stead, different is not bad, it's just different.

5. Seeing God's Image in Others Helps Us See His Image in Ourselves

Scripture: Matthew 22:39; 1 John 4:20

When I value God's design in others, I become better at valuing His design in me. Love flows in both directions: inward and outward. Here's the core of the matter, self-love and neighbor-love grow from the same soil: the imago dei of God.

6. The Enemy Attacks Identity Because Identity Reveals Destiny

Scripture: John 10:10; Genesis 3:1–5

Satan's earliest strategy was identity distortion: "You will be like God…" But Genesis 1:27 declares we already are like God because we are made in His image. When we forget who we are, we lose how to love who we are. Never forget this, self-love is a shield against spiritual deception.

7. Loving Myself Honors God's Original Design

Scripture: Psalm 139:14; Galatians 5:14

God did not create you to despise yourself or diminish yourself. He created you to reflect His love, His creativity, His purpose, and His glory. This is so right and profound! You were created to reflect the glory of the God that created you! Self-love then becomes spiritual obedience that aligns itself with Scripture.

WEEK *Two* TAKEAWAYS

By the end of Week Two, students should confidently affirm:

- "I love myself because God created me in His image." (Genesis 1:27)
- "My worth is not earned, it is inherited from my Creator." (Psalm 8:5)
- "I honor God when I honor His design in me." (Ephesians 2:10)

- "My identity is rooted in creation, not comparison." (Psalm 139:14)
- "Every person, including me, reflects something of God." (James 3:9)

This week was not about loving self from pride, it was about loving self from purpose. Not about inflating the ego, but about celebrating the image of God you carry. Not about self-centeredness, but about theocentric identity.

WEEK *Two* FINAL PRAYER

Lord, thank You for creating me in Your image. Thank You for giving me worth, dignity, and purpose before I ever took a breath. Teach me to see myself as You see me. Heal every place where I have rejected, ignored, or diminished Your image in me. Help me to love myself with the same grace, kindness, and truth that You love me with. As I honor Your design in me, help me honor Your design in others. Thank You for making me fearfully, wonderfully, and intentionally.

In the name of Jesus, Amen!

SECTION I - *Week Three*

DAY 1: THE GROUP ENCOUNTER

THERE'S NOTHING LIKE LOVING ME!

Scripture Lesson: Psalms 139:14

Today's Subject: I'M ONE OF A KIND!

KEY POINTS FROM TODAY'S LESSON

Point 1

_____

_____

_____

_____

_____

Point 2

_____

_____

_____

_____

_____

_____

Point 3

_____

_____

_____

_____

_____

Here's What I'm Praying For Right Now:

_____

_____

_____

_____

_____

_____

_____

_____

DAY 2: "Built for This"

STRAIGHT FROM THE BOOK

"I will praise thee; for I am fearfully and wonderfully made: marvellous are thy works; and that my soul knoweth right well."

(Psalm 139:14, KJV)

JESUS SAID IT BEST

Life can make you question your strength, but Jesus reminds us that we're built by divine design. Every struggle you've survived is proof of the craftsmanship of God. He didn't just make you beautiful, He made you durable. Being fearfully and wonderfully made means you've got Heaven's hardware built into your soul. When Jesus said, "In this world you'll have tribulation, but be of good cheer," He was saying, "You're built for this."

PASTOR PUTS IT LIKE THIS

You've been through hell and came out holy! You've been knocked down, but not knocked out. That's proof that you're built different. Some people would've lost their mind if they went through what you did. But you're still standing, still worshiping, still winning. That's God's construction at work. You're living, breathing evidence that Heaven knows how to build survivors.

THINK ABOUT IT FOR A MOMENT

- What have I survived that shows God's strength in me?
- "Tough times reveal divine design."
- You're not fragile, you're fortified.

PRAY ABOUT IT

Lord, thank You for making me strong in You. Remind me that I'm built to endure and equipped to overcome.

In the name of Jesus, Amen!

DAY 3: "God's Work In Progress"

STRAIGHT FROM THE BOOK

> **"I will praise thee; for I am fearfully and wonderfully made: marvellous are thy works; and that my soul knoweth right well."**

(Psalm 139:14, KJV)

JESUS SAID IT BEST

Jesus didn't pick perfect people, He picked people He would walk through a process. Peter had a temper, Thomas had doubts, and James had ambition, but Jesus still used them. Being fearfully and wonderfully made doesn't mean you're flawless. However, it does mean that you're forming. God's still sculpting your character and maturing your mind. Progress is proof that His hands are still on you.

PASTOR PUTS IT LIKE THIS

Let me bless you: you're not a failure, you're a fixer-upper! God's not done working on you yet. Every day He's sanding off the rough edges and adding polish to your purpose. Don't judge yourself mid-process. You might be "under construction," but the end result is going to be breathtaking. Stay on the Potter's wheel! He knows what He's shaping.

THINK ABOUT IT FOR A MOMENT

- Where do I see God still working in me?
- "Process doesn't mean punishment, it means purpose."
- Don't quit while God's still crafting.

PRAY ABOUT IT

Lord, thank You for being patient with me while You shape me. I trust Your process even when I can't see the progress.

In the name of Jesus, Amen!

DAY 4: "I'm the Evidence"

STRAIGHT FROM THE BOOK

"I will praise thee; for I am fearfully and wonderfully made: marvellous are thy works; and that my soul knoweth right well."

(Psalm 139:14, KJV)

JESUS SAID IT BEST

Every healed scar, every answered prayer, every closed door that turned into a blessing, that's evidence. You're living proof that God is still creating masterpieces from messes. Jesus told His disciples, "let your light so shine before men," because your life is supposed to be visible evidence of His power. When people see you, they should see grace in motion.

PASTOR PUTS IT LIKE THIS

When you look back over your life and realize you made it out of stuff that should've taken you out, you've got to say, "I'm the evidence!" You're the receipt that grace paid it all. You're the proof that mercy still works. Stop hiding your story, somebody needs to see what survival looks like when God's in it.

THINK ABOUT IT FOR A MOMENT

- What parts of my life prove God's power is real?
- "Your testimony is somebody else's survival guide."
- Don't hide your evidence, put it on display.

PRAY ABOUT IT

Lord, thank You for making my life a living testimony. Help me to share my story with boldness so others can see Your hand on me.

In the name of Jesus, Amen!

DAY 5: "Flaws and All"

STRAIGHT FROM THE BOOK

"I will praise thee; for I am fearfully and wonderfully made: marvellous are thy works; and that my soul knoweth right well."

(Psalm 139:14, KJV)

JESUS SAID IT BEST

When Jesus called people to follow Him, He didn't wait for them to get perfect first. He embraced their flaws and still gave them a future. Loving yourself "flaws and all" means seeing your imperfections as opportunities for grace. Keep this in mind, Jesus never said or spoke the term grace, not once! Instead of speaking it, He was so full of it He made it impossible for you to miss. God's beauty shows up best through broken people who must have grace to survive. The cracks in your story let His light of grace shine through.

PASTOR PUTS IT LIKE THIS

We all got something! Don't let your flaws make you forget your favor. Even your struggles serve a purpose. Diamonds shine because of pressure. Stop apologizing for being human, God already factored in your flaws when He called you. You may not be perfect, but you're perfectly placed in His plan. In other words, do not try to model perfection, show the world redemption and boast openly on the grace of God and what it produces.

THINK ABOUT IT FOR A MOMENT

- Can I thank God even for the parts of me I don't like?
- "Grace looks good on me."
- Perfection is overrated; authenticity is anointed.

PRAY ABOUT IT

Lord, thank You for loving me, flaws and all. Help me to see beauty where I used to see brokenness.

In The Name of Jesus, Amen!

DAY 6: "Made for More"

STRAIGHT FROM THE BOOK

"I will praise thee; for I am fearfully and wonderfully made: marvellous are thy works; and that my soul knoweth right well."

(Psalm 139:14, KJV)

JESUS SAID IT BEST

Jesus said, "greater works shall ye do." That means there's more in you than what you've seen. Being fearfully and wonderfully made means God packed your potential with purpose. Potential is best defined as what you could do that you haven't done yet. Potential is untapped strength, unused victory and unwon battles! Don't settle for small thinking or safe dreams. The same God who designed galaxies designed you, so dream big, love hard, and walk tall.

PASTOR PUTS IT LIKE THIS

You were made for more than just bills, breaks, and burnout! You were made to build, bless, and believe. There's greatness sitting inside you like uncashed checks. Stop living beneath your birthright. God didn't make you basic, He made you boundless. Step into your "more" with boldness and faith.

THINK ABOUT IT FOR A MOMENT

- What "more" is God calling me toward right now?
- "You're not done, you're developing."
- Don't shrink for people who fear your future.

PRAY ABOUT IT

Lord, thank You for making me for more. Ignite my passion, fuel my purpose, and push me into every promise You've written with my name on it.

In the name of Jesus, Amen!

DAY 7: "God's Masterpiece"

STRAIGHT FROM THE BOOK

"I will praise thee; for I am fearfully and wonderfully made: marvellous are thy works; and that my soul knoweth right well."

(Psalm 139:14, KJV)

JESUS SAID IT BEST

When Jesus came, He showed us what divine design looks like in flesh: intentional, excellent, and holy. God doesn't do random, He does remarkable! Every feature of your life was crafted with care. Being "fearfully and wonderfully made" means God put reverence and wonder into your creation. Here's the great news of the day: you're not just another face in the crowd, you are evidence of God's divine design.

PASTOR PUTS IT LIKE THIS

You're not a factory product, you're fine art! God handcrafted you. That's why no one else can do you like you do you. You're a one of one! You're not a cheap duplicate, you're a priceless original. Stop trying to copy somebody else's style when God already gave you your own signature. You're the remix God was excited to release! Stand tall and own your design!

THINK ABOUT IT FOR A MOMENT

- What makes me unique in God's plan?
- "You're not an accident, you're an assignment."
- Confidence starts when you stop apologizing for being you.

PRAY ABOUT IT

Lord, thank You for making me Your masterpiece. Help me to see myself through Your creative eyes and not through comparison.

In the name of Jesus, Amen!

CONCLUSION | Week Three | "FEARFULLY AND WONDERFULLY MADE"

As We Conclude Week Three...

This week, our hearts rested on the powerful truth found in Psalm 139:14:

"I will praise Thee; for I am fearfully and wonderfully made..."

We learned that loving ourselves is not rooted in pride, ego, or culture, it is rooted in praise. David teaches us that self-worth begins not with self-esteem, but with how God-esteems you. The more clearly we see God's greatness, the more confidently we embrace our own value. This week has taught us that God designed us intentionally, uniquely, and beautifully, and that loving ourselves is an act of worship toward the One who made us.

Below is a biblical summation of what students should now understand after studying together.

WHAT WE LEARNED THIS WEEK

1. God Made You With Intention, Not Indifference

Scripture: Psalm 139:14; Jeremiah 1:5

You are fearfully made — meaning carefully, skillfully, purposefully crafted by God. You are not random. You are not accidental. You are not an afterthought. Your existence was planned in eternity.

2. God Designed You With Beauty, Value, and Excellence

Scripture: Genesis 1:31; Ephesians 2:10

"Wonderfully made" means you were created with delight and distinction. God celebrated your creation. He approved of you. He called you "good." Your worth is built into your design.

3. Self-Love Is an Act of Worship, Not Pride

Scripture: Psalm 139:14; Proverbs 3:6

David ties self-recognition to praise, "I will praise Thee, for I am wonderfully made."

When you honor God's creation in yourself, you are honoring God Himself. Self-love isn't arrogance, it's agreement!

4. God's Works Are Marvelous, Including You

Scripture: Psalm 139:14; Job 10:12

David says, "marvelous are Thy works," and YOU are one of those works. Loving yourself means recognizing the miracle of your existence. There is nothing ordinary about a child of God.

5. Self-Worth Must Be Rooted in What Your Soul "Knows Right Well"

Scripture: Psalm 139:14; Romans 8:16

Your emotions may lie. People may cause damage. Culture may confuse. But your soul knows: God made you! God values you. God delights in you. Self-love becomes stronger when it is built on what the soul knows, not what the world says.

6. The Enemy Attacks What God Affirms

Scripture: John 10:10; Psalm 139:1–4

Satan attacks identity, worth, and self-view because he hates anything God celebrates. If you feel unworthy, unloved, unseen, or not enough just know that those feelings contradict Scripture. The enemy wants to destroy what God designed; self-love protects what God created.

7. Loving Yourself Helps You Love Others Correctly

Scripture: Matthew 22:39; 1 John 4:20

How you see yourself affects how you see everyone else. If you believe you are fearfully and wonderfully made, you can recognize that same divine craftsmanship in others. Self-love is the foundation of relational love.

WEEK *Three* TAKEAWAYS

By the end of Week Three, students should confidently affirm:

- "I am fearfully and wonderfully made." (Psalm 139:14)
- "God's craftsmanship is evident in my life." (Ephesians 2:10)
- "I honor God when I honor what He created." (Genesis 1:31)
- "My value is intrinsic, not earned." (Jeremiah 1:5)
- "My soul knows I am God's masterpiece." (Psalm 139:14)

This week was not about hyping the ego. It was about healing the identity. Not about celebrating self, but celebrating the God who made you. Not about self-promotion, but self-recognition according to Scripture.

WEEK *Three* FINAL PRAYER

Lord, thank You for making me fearfully and wonderfully made. Thank You for the intentional detail, value, and design You placed in my life. Help me see myself through Your eyes. Heal every wound that has damaged my self-worth. Silence every voice that contradicts Your truth. Teach me to love myself in a way that honors You. Let my soul rest in what it knows right well, that I am Your creation, Your masterpiece, and Your beloved.

In the name of Jesus, Amen.

SECTION I - *Week Four*

DAY 1: THE GROUP ENCOUNTER

THERE'S NOTHING LIKE LOVING ME!

Scripture Lesson: Ephesians 2:10

Today's Subject: PARDON THE DUST, HE'S MAKING SOME IMPROVEMENTS!

KEY POINTS FROM TODAY'S LESSON

Point 1

_____

_____

_____

_____

_____

Point 2

_____

_____

_____

_____

_____

_____

Point 3

_____

_____

_____

_____

_____

_____

Here's What I'm Praying For Right Now:

_____

_____

_____

_____

_____

_____

_____

_____

DAY 2: "Born for Greatness"

STRAIGHT FROM THE BOOK

"For we are his workmanship, created in Christ Jesus unto good works, which God hath before ordained that we should walk in them." (Ephesians 2:10 (KJV)

JESUS SAID IT BEST

Jesus constantly reminded His followers that they were created for "greater works." You were made for more than mediocrity. You were designed for greatness. Being God's workmanship means that excellence is in your blueprint. God didn't save you to sit still; He saved you to shine. Here's the best news of the day, the greatness in you was designed for you to be the light of the world.

PASTOR PUTS IT LIKE THIS

You've got greatness in your DNA! You were born to bring change, not chase clout. Stop sleeping on who God is making you to become. The Lord put gifts in you the world hasn't seen yet. You don't need permission to be great when you've already got purpose. Walk tall, talk faith, and remember that greatness is not arrogance; it's obedience.

THINK ABOUT IT FOR A MOMENT

- Where am I playing small when God called me to stand tall?
- "Don't apologize for shining when God turned the light on."
- You were born for it. Act like it.

PRAY ABOUT IT

Lord, thank You for planting greatness in me. Help me to walk boldly in the purpose You ordained for my life.

In the name of Jesus, Amen!

DAY 3: "Grace Made Me"

STRAIGHT FROM THE BOOK

> "For we are his workmanship, created in Christ Jesus unto good works, which God hath before ordained that we should walk in them." (Ephesians 2:10 (KJV)

JESUS SAID IT BEST

Jesus never mentioned the word grace one time in the Greek New Testament. However, like an architect, He built everything He touched with it. He took broken pieces and made them whole again. He took the blind and gave them sight. He took the lame and made them walk. Now here's the shout, that's the foundation of our identity, grace made me. Your worth isn't based on your wins or your works; it's based on Christ finished work on the cross. In other words, you're not self-made, you're Savior-made.

PASTOR PUTS IT LIKE THIS

Some people like to brag about being "self-made." This is not my claim. God's grace made me! Every success I've had is stamped by mercy only. Please know, you didn't earn this favor; it was given to you. That's why you can walk in confidence without arrogance. It's not about you, it's about Him working through you.

THINK ABOUT IT FOR A MOMENT

- What in my life reminds me that grace made me?
- "If grace built it, hell can't break it."
- Your resume didn't make you. God's gracious redemption did.

PRAY ABOUT IT

Lord, thank You that I am who I am by Your grace. Help me to live grateful for what You've made me to be.

In the name of Jesus, Amen!

DAY 4: "Purpose Over Popularity"

STRAIGHT FROM THE BOOK

"For we are his workmanship, created in Christ Jesus unto good works, which God hath before ordained that we should walk in them." (Ephesians 2:10 (KJV)

JESUS SAID IT BEST

As social media influence surges, it is common for people to do just about anything to gain popularity. However, let it be known, Jesus Christ never chased fame. He fulfilled His purpose. While crowds sought miracles, He sought the will of His Father. Being God's workmanship means your value isn't found in being known by people, but being used by God. Popularity fades, but purpose fulfills.

PASTOR PUTS IT LIKE THIS

You don't need likes to be loved or followers to be fulfilled. You're already verified in Heaven! In other words, when God called you, He didn't check with Instagram first. Stay focused on what He is calling you to do. You will discover, that's what lasts forever. Let other people chase attention; you chase the assignment. That's where real popularity lives.

THINK ABOUT IT FOR A MOMENT

- Am I living for applause or assignment?
- "Purpose doesn't need promotion, just obedience."
- Don't do it just for the likes, do it because you love it.

PRAY ABOUT IT

Lord, keep me grounded in purpose, not distracted by popularity. Let me live to please You, not to impress people.

In the name of Jesus, Amen!

DAY 5: "He's Still Working on Me"

STRAIGHT FROM THE BOOK

"For we are his workmanship, created in Christ Jesus unto good works, which God hath before ordained that we should walk in them." (Ephesians 2:10 (KJV)

JESUS SAID IT BEST

People, who are not Christians, often peep through church windows and decide not to join the church because they see no finished products in attendance, including the preacher. However, get this, even Jesus grew "in wisdom and stature." That means development is divine. You are God's ongoing project, constantly being refined, reshaped, and renewed. His workmanship is still in motion, turning raw potential into a finished project. Every day He cuts some things away. He gets rid of stuff in you that's not like Him.

PASTOR PUTS IT LIKE THIS

Be patient, God's still got His powerful hands on you. You might not like the process, but it's part of becoming a masterpiece. The Potter doesn't throw the clay away halfway through. He keeps molding until it looks right. So when life feels rough, just remember: construction means progress.

THINK ABOUT IT FOR A MOMENT

- Where do I feel God still shaping me?
- "Unfinished doesn't mean unworthy."
- The process proves His presence.

PRAY ABOUT IT

Lord, thank You for never giving up on me. Keep working until I look like what You dreamed when You made me.

In the name of Jesus, Amen!

DAY 6: "The Finished Product"

STRAIGHT FROM THE BOOK

"For we are his workmanship, created in Christ Jesus unto good works, which God hath before ordained that we should walk in them." (Ephesians 2:10 (KJV)

JESUS SAID IT BEST

Jesus spoke seven words from the cross. One of which was *Te Telestai*. It translates into English as "it is finished." These weren't words of defeat. They were the declaration of an assignment fulfilled. The good news about these words is this, when He finished His work, He also completed yours. Being God's workmanship means the victory is already written. Your story doesn't end in failure. It ends in fulfillment. You're not working for approval, you're working from it.

PASTOR PUTS IT LIKE THIS

When Jesus said, "it is finished," He placed a check mark by your name which meant the entire project is "complete." Jesus paid it all! It is a done deal! That's a wrap! You're the finished product of His grace. So walk like it! You've already got the victory, the favor, and the identity. The masterpiece is done, now it's time to put it on display!

THINK ABOUT IT FOR A MOMENT

- What does it mean to live like God's finished work?
- "You're not chasing victory, you're walking in it."
- Completion feels like peace.

PRAY ABOUT IT

Lord, thank You that through Christ, my story is complete. Help me live boldly as Your finished masterpiece.

In the name of Jesus, Amen!

DAY 7: "Walk It Out"

STRAIGHT FROM THE BOOK

> **"For we are his workmanship, created in Christ Jesus unto good works, which God hath before ordained that we should walk in them. (Ephesians 2:10, KJV)**

JESUS SAID IT BEST

Jesus didn't just talk the talk, He walked the walk. Everywhere He went, love and kingdom purpose followed Him. The power of being God's workmanship is not just knowing who you are, but walking it out daily. It's one thing to believe you're made by God; it's another to live like it. Jesus lived intentionally, every step, every word, every move reflected His Father's divine design. Now here's the shout of the day, that's how we turn our divine design into daily direction.

PASTOR PUTS IT LIKE THIS

Let me break it down, it's time to walk it like you talk it! You're God's masterpiece, not a statue in a museum. That means you don't just sit pretty, you move with purpose, passion and power. Every day you wake up, walk in confidence, in peace, in love, in prayer. Let your life be a runway where God's grace struts His stuff through you! Do not try to show the world perfection, but show them what redemption looks like!

THINK ABOUT IT FOR A MOMENT

- What would it look like if I walked out what I believe every day?
- "Faith without movement is just good intentions."
- When purpose walks in, fear walks out.

PRAY ABOUT IT

Lord, help me to walk boldly in the purpose You created for me. Let every step I take represent the masterpiece You made me to be.

In the name of Jesus, Amen!

CONCLUSION | Week Four | EPHESIANS 2:10

As We Conclude Week Four...

This week we discovered the rich biblical truth found in Ephesians 2:10 (KJV):

"For we are his workmanship, created in Christ Jesus unto good works, which God hath before ordained that we should walk in them."

Believers, in Christ Jesus, should now understand that their identity is anchored in God's intentional design. Their purpose is rooted in His eternal plan. Their lives are shaped by the One who calls them His masterpiece. We are not random. We are not accidental. We are God-crafted, Christ-created, and Spirit-empowered to live out good works that reveal His glory.

WHAT WE LEARNED THIS WEEK

1. We Are God's Workmanship

We learned that the word workmanship translates from the Greek poiēmon, meaning "masterpiece," "poem," or "a work of art." This means our existence reflects God's creativity, intentionality, and personal touch (Psalm 139:14).

2. We Were Created in Christ Jesus

This week taught us that salvation reshapes us from the inside out. In Christ, we are new creations with a restored identity and a renewed purpose (2 Corinthians 5:17).

3. We Were Made for Good Works

We discovered that good works are not a path to salvation, but the fruit of salvation. They reveal God's love, demonstrate His character, and influence the world around us (Matthew 5:16).

4. God Prepared Our Purpose in Advance

We learned that purpose begins with God, not with us. Before we ever existed, God designed a path for our lives. Our steps are guided by His wisdom. Our destiny is secured in His hands (Jeremiah 29:11).

5. We Are Called to Walk in God's Plan

This week showed us that purpose is lived out daily through obedience, trust, and alignment with God's will (Proverbs 3:5–6). We walk out what God has already worked out.

WEEK *Four* TAKE AWAYS

- I am God's masterpiece, not a mistake.
- My value comes from God's design, not people's opinions.
- My purpose was prepared before I was born.
- Good works are God's way of expressing Himself through my life.
- Walking with God shapes my identity, strengthens my faith, and clarifies my direction.
- I am created with intentionality, redeemed with purpose, and sent out with assignment.

WEEK *Four* FINAL PRAYER

Father, thank You for calling us Your workmanship. Thank You for creating us in Christ Jesus and preparing good works for us long before we walked this earth. Guide our steps as we live out Your purpose for our lives. Help us see ourselves the way You see us: valuable, intentional, and highly favored. Strengthen us to walk boldly in the plans You have ordained. Let our lives reflect Your glory in every word, action, and decision.

In Jesus' name, Amen.

SECTION II - *Week One*

DAY 1: THE GROUP ENCOUNTER

THERE'S NOTHING LIKE LOVING YOU!

Scripture Lesson: St. John. 13:34

Today's Subject: IT'S THE TRADEMARK!

KEY POINTS FROM TODAY'S LESSON

Point 1

_____

_____

_____

_____

_____

Point 2

_____

_____

_____

_____

_____

Point 3

_____

_____

_____

_____

_____

_____

Here's What I'm Praying For Right Now:

_____

_____

_____

_____

_____

_____

_____

_____

_____

DAY 2: "Love on Command"

STRAIGHT FROM THE BOOK

"A new commandment I give unto you, That ye love one another; as I have loved you, that ye also love one another." (John 13:34, KJV)

JESUS SAID IT BEST

Love is so powerful in the Kingdom of God that the Lord actually defines Himself as such. In short, God is love. When Jesus told His disciples to "….love one another…", He didn't offer a suggestion, He gave a command. Love isn't optional in the Kingdom; it's essential. He didn't say "love the ones who love you back." He said, "love one another as I have loved you." That means love that forgives, heals, and restores.

PASTOR PUTS IT LIKE THIS

Okay, let's be real for a moment, some people are hard to love. And, if we'd be honest, there are others that make love feel like hard work in the hot Texas sun in the summer heat! But Jesus didn't give us a loophole. He gave us a law: love like He did. That means loving when it's inconvenient, when it's uncomfortable, when it's unreciprocated and unappreciated. You're never more like Jesus than when you love somebody that does not love you.

THINK ABOUT IT FOR A MOMENT

- Who in my life is God challenging me to love better?
- "Obedience is the first act of love."
- Love is not a mood; it's a move.

PRAY ABOUT IT

Lord, help me to obey Your command to love others as You love me, even when it's not easy.

In the name of Jesus, Amen!

DAY 3: "Unfollow the Hate"

STRAIGHT FROM THE BOOK

"**A new commandment I give unto you, That ye love one another; as I have loved you, that ye also love one another.**" **(John 13:34, KJV)**

JESUS SAID IT BEST

Jesus taught us that love breaks cycles, especially the cycle of hate. When He commanded love, He was giving His followers a way out of revenge and resentment. Real love doesn't repost hate, it replaces it.

PASTOR PUTS IT LIKE THIS

Okay, so here's the truth, some of us need to hit that "unfollow" button, not on social media, but in our spiritual mindsets. Unfollow bitterness. Unfollow grudges. Unfollow hatred. Unfollow unforgiveness. Unfollow resentment. Unfollow that old offense you've been replaying in your mind. You can't carry hate and holiness at the same time. Let love lead, and let the rest go. Hear this simple command because it just makes sense, let it go!

THINK ABOUT IT FOR A MOMENT

- What hate have I been holding onto that God wants me to release?
- "You can't heal while you're still hating."
- Love sets you free faster than anger ever will.

PRAY ABOUT IT

Lord, help me unfollow hate and walk in forgiveness. Free my heart to love without limits.

In the name of Jesus, Amen!

DAY 4: "Love Ain't Scared"

STRAIGHT FROM THE BOOK

"A new commandment I give unto you, That ye love one another; as I have loved you, that ye also love one another." (John 13:34, KJV)

JESUS SAID IT BEST

The most dynamic part of the earthly ministry of Jesus Christ was not His ability to heal. It was His ability to love! Jesus loved boldly. He loved lepers, tax collectors, and traitors. He loved the lovable, the unloveable, the evil, the mean and the hateful. He never let fear dictate His compassion. Perfect love casts out fear! Here's the truth, real love steps into uncomfortable spaces and makes the difference every time.

PASTOR PUTS IT LIKE THIS

Here's a moment that requires more than honesty, but total transparency. There are times when we hold back love and hold on to bitterness and grudges because we're scared of being hurt again. But fear and love can't live in the same space. Where fear lives, love will never abide. In short, here's the root of the matter, love ain't scared, it's strong. Don't let past pain make you petty. When you love like Jesus, you win even when your haters walk away.

THINK ABOUT IT FOR A MOMENT

- What fear keeps me from loving freely?
- "Fear builds walls. Love builds bridges."
- Loving big requires living brave.

PRAY ABOUT IT

Lord, give me the courage to love fearlessly and the faith to trust You with my heart.

In the name of Jesus, Amen!

DAY 5: "Love Looks Like Something"

STRAIGHT FROM THE BOOK

> "**A new commandment I give unto you, That ye love one another; as I have loved you, that ye also love one another.**" (**John 13:34, KJV**)

JESUS SAID IT BEST

Jesus didn't just talk about love, He demonstrated it. He washed feet, fed the hungry, healed the hurting, and forgave the guilty. Love always has a look, a sound, and a sacrifice. When He said, "love one another," He meant show it.

PASTOR PUTS IT LIKE THIS

Love, without action attached, is like a car without an engine. It's going nowhere really fast. Love without action attached is a pizza with no bread, sauce, wings or pepperoni! In other words, don't just say you love people, show them! Love looks like forgiveness, kindness, patience, care, concern, and generosity. Wait, please understand this, love is not rooted in stupidity, but humility! As a believer in Jesus Christ, you love because it's what the Lord has commanded and not because it's something you feel like doing.

THINK ABOUT IT FOR A MOMENT

- How can I make love visible today?
- "Love unspoken is love unfinished."
- If Jesus' love had a look, so should yours.

PRAY ABOUT IT

Lord, help my love to be more than words. Let it be visible, tangible, touchable and life-giving to others.

In the name of Jesus, Amen!

DAY 6: "Keep That Same Energy"

STRAIGHT FROM THE BOOK

> "A new commandment I give unto you, That ye love one another; as I have loved you, that ye also love one another." (John 13:34, KJV)

JESUS SAID IT BEST

Jesus' love was consistent. He didn't love people on Monday and ghost them by Friday. His love was steady through storms, betrayal, and even death. Real love doesn't change with moods or moments because it's anchored in God's grace.

PASTOR PUTS IT LIKE THIS

As a Pastor, I often encounter people who start off good after hearing a sermon and before the week is out, their love for those that are difficult is gone. A new grudge has replaced the old one. In short, we're great at starting with love, but we are short with staying in love. We love folks until they mess up, disagree, or disappoint us. Jesus kept that same vibe all the way to the cross! Okay so here's the meat of today's message, if the Lord didn't give up on you, don't give up on them. Love them through it.

THINK ABOUT IT FOR A MOMENT

- Where have I stopped loving because it got hard?
- "Consistency is the proof of real love."
- Love that lasts looks like loyalty.

PRAY ABOUT IT

Lord, teach me how to love with endurance, not just emotion. Help me to stay faithful in love, just like You.

In the name of Jesus, Amen!

DAY 7: "Love in Real Time"

STRAIGHT FROM THE BOOK

"**A new commandment I give unto you, That ye love one another; as I have loved you, that ye also love one another.**" **(John 13:34, KJV)**

JESUS SAID IT BEST

Love, that's delayed, can become love that's denied. Jesus loved in real time. He loved when people needed it the most and not when it was convenient. Christ-like love acts now, speaks now, forgives now. That's how lives change, not by waiting for the right time, but by realizing that the right time is right now!

PASTOR PUTS IT LIKE THIS

By now, I realize that this lesson is putting the squeeze on many of you. The reason for this is because loving some people is extremely difficult for you! It is much easier for you to tell people; "just stay out of my face!" I have even heard people say, "I'll forgive them one day, but not today because I'm just not ready!" However, hear the Word of the Lord. Make up your mind to love today and just do it! Forgive them today. Release the hurt today. You are one decision away from healing and it starts with you making a decision for love!

THINK ABOUT IT FOR A MOMENT

- Who needs my love today, not tomorrow?
- "Love delayed is help denied."
- Don't wait to say it, show it.

PRAY ABOUT IT

Lord, help me love in real time. Help me be quick to act, quick to forgive, quick to serve. Please help my love act like Yours.

In the name of Jesus, Amen!

CONCLUSION | Week One | ST. JOHN 13:34

As We Conclude Week One...

This week, our study centered on the powerful command Jesus gives His disciples in St. John 13:34 (KJV):

"A new commandment I give unto you, That ye love one another; as I have loved you, that ye also love one another."

Throughout this week, we learned that Christian love is not optional, it is essential. Jesus lifts love beyond emotion and preference, establishing His own love for us as the model we must follow. Believers in the Lord Jesus Christ should now understand that Christlike love is the identifying mark of discipleship and the foundation for all Christian living.

WHAT WE LEARNED THIS WEEK

1. Jesus Gives Us a New Command Rooted in His Own Love (John 13:34)

We learned that Jesus raises the standard of love. The command is "new" because it calls us to love others with the same depth, sacrifice, and commitment that He demonstrates toward us.

2. Christ's Love Becomes the Standard for All Relationships

Our love is measured not by how we feel, but by how Jesus loves. His love is patient, forgiving, humble, and consistent (Ephesians 4:2).

3. Love Identifies Us as True Disciples (John 13:35)

We discovered that love is the visible proof of our relationship with Jesus. When believers love one another, the world sees evidence of Christ at work in us.

4. Christlike Love Requires Action, Not Intention Alone

We learned that love must be demonstrated. Like Jesus washing His disciples' feet, we are called to serve with humility and compassion (John 13:14–15).

5. Loving Others Reflects God's Character to the World

This week showed us that God is revealed through our relationships. When we love others well, we display the heart of God (1 John 4:12).

IMPORTANT WEEK *One* TAKEAWAYS

- I am commanded, not suggested, to love others as Christ has loved me.
- Christ's love is the model, measure, and motivation for all my relationships.
- My love for others reveals my identity as a disciple of Jesus.
- True love requires humility, patience, forgiveness, and service.
- I cannot love well without first receiving and reflecting the love of Christ.
- Love builds unity, heals brokenness, and strengthens Christian community.
- When I love others, I participate in showing God to the world.

WEEK *One* FINAL PRAYER

Lord Jesus, thank You for commanding us to love one another as You have loved us. As we conclude this week's study, empower us to live out this command daily. Teach us to love with humility, patience, compassion and sincerity. Remove anything within us that hinders tolerance, forbearance and unity. Let our lives reflect Your heart, and let our love point others to Your saving grace. Shape our character, strengthen our relationships, and mold us into true disciples who walk in Your love.

In the name of Jesus, Amen.

SECTION II - *Week Two*

DAY 1: THE GROUP ENCOUNTER

THERE'S NOTHING LIKE LOVING YOU!

Scripture Lesson: 1 John 4:7

Today's Subject: I'VE GOT PROOF!

KEY POINTS FROM TODAY'S LESSON

Point 1

_____

_____

_____

_____

_____

Point 2

_____

_____

_____

_____

_____

Point 3

_____

_____

_____

_____

_____

_____

Here's What I'm Praying For Right Now:

_____

_____

_____

_____

_____

_____

_____

DAY 2: "Love Is the Family Trait"

STRAIGHT FROM THE BOOK

"Beloved, let us love one another: for love is of God; and every one that loveth is born of God, and knoweth God." (1 John 4:7, KJV)

JESUS SAID IT BEST

John reminds us that love isn't just an act, it is our newfound identity in Jesus Christ. To be "born of God" means to carry the spiritual DNA of God running in your veins. We know this to be true because God's primary attribute is love. Jesus said, "by this all men will know you're my disciples, if you have love one to another." When people encounter us, they should recognize who our Father is by how we treat one another.

PASTOR PUTS IT LIKE THIS

I tell the Antioch Church every Sunday that people decide to unite with the church because of the love they receive from the people seated in the pew. When believers demonstrate love, those who do not have a church home or have not come to know Jesus Christ find themselves drawing nigh to God because of the love they have experienced and encountered. In other words, you've heard people say, "you look just like your daddy"? Well, when you love people, Heaven says the same thing! Love is the family resemblance of God's children. If you claim the bloodline of Christ, you've got to carry His heart. Don't let hate make you forget your heritage. You were born into a loving family, so act like it!

THINK ABOUT IT FOR A MOMENT

- Do I look like my Father in how I love?
- "If God is love, His kids should look like it."
- Love proves my spiritual birth certificate.

PRAY ABOUT IT

Lord, thank You for making me part of Your family. Help me reflect Your heart in how I treat others today.

In the name of Jesus, Amen!

DAY 3: "God's Kind of Love"

STRAIGHT FROM THE BOOK

> **"Beloved, let us love one another: for love is of God; and every one that loveth is born of God, and knoweth God." (1 John 4:7, KJV)**

JESUS SAID IT BEST

God's love isn't fragile or flaky, it's faithful. His love doesn't depend on mood swings, mistakes, or merit. That's the "agape" love John is talking about in the study passage for the week. It is a love that gives without expecting anything back. Jesus lived that kind of love on the cross. The cross of our Christ is proof positive that He loved not just some of us, but all of us beyond decree.

PASTOR PUTS IT LIKE THIS

So here's a moment of radical truth, most of us were taught conditional love: "I love you if you do right by me." But God flips that. He says, "I love you even when you don't." This kind of love moves mountains, changes lives and converts sinners to produce saints. That's the kind of love that changes people, breaks generational curses, and heals hearts. So here's the challenge, don't just love like the culture and the people around us; love like Christ.

THINK ABOUT IT FOR A MOMENT

- What does it look like to love like God loves?
- "Real love gives and the shout is that it doesn't keep score."
- Love that costs nothing usually changes nothing.

PRAY ABOUT IT

Lord, teach me how to love with Your kind of love: patient, powerful, and pure.

In the name of Jesus, Amen!

DAY 4: "Born to Love"

STRAIGHT FROM THE BOOK

"Beloved, let us love one another: for love is of God; and every one that loveth is born of God, and knoweth God." (1 John 4:7, KJV)

JESUS SAID IT BEST

Fish are born to swim. Lions are born to roar. A cheetah is born with speed and some birds are born to fly. But, when a believer is born-again, we are born to love. John teaches that love isn't something you learn from the world, it's something you inherit from Heaven. To be "born of God" is to be born for love. Jesus proved that when He loved the least, the lost, the left out, and the left behind.

PASTOR PUTS IT LIKE THIS

Here's the shout for this week's lesson, you were born to do this! Love is not your weakness, it's your weapon. When folks hate on you, don't let them drag you out of character. You were born to love, not to match their mess, their madness and their foolishness. Remember, when you love right, you fight right.

THINK ABOUT IT FOR A MOMENT

- How often do I choose love over reacting?
- "When I know who I am, I know how to love."
- Love isn't learned behavior; it's divine DNA.

PRAY ABOUT IT

Lord, thank You for giving me Your heart at my new birth. Help me love from who I am, not what I feel.

In the name of Jesus, Amen!

DAY 5: "The Love Test"

STRAIGHT FROM THE BOOK

"Beloved, let us love one another: for love is of God; and every one that loveth is born of God, and knoweth God." (1 John 4:7, KJV)

JESUS SAID IT BEST

God never ever tempts believers; but, He does test us. John says, love is the evidence of knowing God. That means, the real test of spiritual maturity isn't how well you quote Scripture, but it's how well you love people. Jesus said, "if you love Me, feed My sheep." Loving people is how we prove that our relationship with Him is real.

PASTOR PUTS IT LIKE THIS

There are those of us who think that the "love test" is optional, but it's actually an open book daily examination! God's grading scale is not based on how loud you sing, it's based on how deep you love. You can pass every class in theological seminary and still fail in compassion. Please hear this with your whole heart, don't flunk love! Christ-like love is the game changer!

THINK ABOUT IT FOR A MOMENT

- Who has God placed in my life as my "love test"?
- "Love is the only exam you take every day."
- How you treat people is your real praise report.

PRAY ABOUT IT

Lord, don't let me fail the love test. Let my words, actions, and responses all reflect Your heart.

In the name of Jesus, Amen!

DAY 6: "Love in Motion"

STRAIGHT FROM THE BOOK

"Beloved, let us love one another: for love is of God; and every one that loveth is born of God, and knoweth God." (1 John 4:7, KJV)

JESUS SAID IT BEST

Have you ever noticed that the ocean never sits still. It's always in motion. A rolling tide, a wave that comes crushing into the seashore. The waters of the ocean move! Like the waters of the ocean move, real love moves. It's not stuck like a chunk of cement. It's expressed in action. Every time Jesus loved someone, something happened: blind eyes opened, broken hearts were healed, lost souls found hope. Love is never passive. It's always powerful in motion.

PASTOR PUTS IT LIKE THIS

Talk can be found on a clearance rack at any Dollar General store, but love is not like that! Love is a high dollar commodity that never ever goes on sale. With this in mind, when you decide to love and to be real with it, you will pay dearly for it! It's not just something that you post on a social media site with a few nice pics to go with it. Love requires a purchase that comes with a sacrifice. In a very real sense, pick up that phone, send that prayer, lend that hand, give that hug. Love is a verb. If it's not moving, it's not love.

THINK ABOUT IT FOR A MOMENT

- Who needs to see my love in motion this week?
- "Love without action is simply false advertisement."
- Motion proves meaning.

PRAY ABOUT IT

Lord, let my love be alive and active. Help me put love to work where it's needed most.

In the name of Jesus, Amen!

DAY 7: "Love Never Loses"

STRAIGHT FROM THE BOOK

"Beloved, let us love one another: for love is of God; and every one that loveth is born of God, and knoweth God." (1 John 4:7, KJV)

JESUS SAID IT BEST

Love always wins! Love never ever loses! Even when it appears to be nailed to a tree, placed in a borrowed tomb, and covered by a huge rock that weighs two tons, it still wins! With this in mind, understand that it's not because love never gets hurt, but because it never gives up! Love never quits! Love is never through loving! When Jesus loved the world enough to die for it, that looked like loss on Good Friday, but love rose victorious on Resurrection Sunday morning. In a Christocentric sense, true love never loses because it's always powered by a life supported by a resurrection.

PASTOR PUTS IT LIKE THIS

The world might think that love is weak, but you and I know it's the strongest force in the whole wide world. Hate runs out of gas, but love refills itself. Keep loving, even when it hurts or even when it's hard. Love cannot fail you. That's why this entire book is about Core Value 2, LOVE!

THINK ABOUT IT FOR A MOMENT

- Where have I stopped loving because I thought it wasn't working?
- "Love may look defeated, but it's never done."
- Love's record is still undefeated.

PRAY ABOUT IT

Lord, thank You for showing me that love never fails. Help me stay faithful to love even when it's not easy.

In the name of Jesus, Amen!

CONCLUSION | WEEK *Two* | 1 JOHN 4:7

As We Conclude Week *Two*...

This week our study centered on the powerful truth found in 1 John 4:7 (KJV):

"Beloved, let us love one another: for love is of God; and every one that loveth is born of God, and knoweth God."

After studying this one verse all week long, you should now understand that love is not simply something God does, love is who God is. And because we are born of Him, we are called to reflect His nature. This week taught us that authentic Christian love flows from a heart transformed by God, strengthened by the Spirit, and rooted in the knowledge of who God is. Love is both our identity and our assignment.

WHAT WE LEARNED THIS WEEK

1. Love Originates with God (1 John 4:7)

We learned that love comes from God Himself. It does not begin with our emotions, preferences, or personality. It begins with God's nature. To know God is to learn the language of love.

2. Everyone Born of God is Empowered to Love

This week revealed that believers love because they carry God's spiritual DNA. Love is evidence of new birth, spiritual maturity, and genuine connection with Christ (1 John 4:7–8).

3. Loving Others Reveals Our Relationship with God

We discovered that love for others is how believers show they truly know God. With this in mind, love is not just a feeling. It is the visible proof of our discipleship (John 13:35).

4. God's Love is the Standard for How We Treat Others

We learned that we do not love from our own strength; we love from God's supply. His love shapes our patience, forgiveness, compassion, and endurance (1 Corinthians 13:4–7).

5. Love is the Mark of a Spirit-Led Life

This week taught us that love is fruit. It is the natural evidence of the Holy Spirit working in us (Galatians 5:22). When we walk with God, we walk in love.

IMPORTANT WEEK *Two* TAKEAWAYS

- Love begins with God and flows through me.
- If I truly know God, my relationships will show it.
- Loving others is not optional — it is evidence of new birth.
- God empowers me to love beyond my own strength.
- Love is the clearest sign of spiritual maturity.
- Loving well is how I reflect God to the world.
- When I choose love, I choose to walk in the Spirit.

WEEK *Two* FINAL PRAYER

Lord, thank You for showing us that love comes from You and flows through us. As we conclude Week Two, help us to love one another with sincerity, strength, and compassion. Let our lives reflect Your heart. Teach us to love beyond emotion and to love through Your Spirit. May every relationship we have reveal that we truly know You. Shape our character, deepen our compassion, and help us walk in love daily. In Jesus' name, Amen.

SECTION II - *Week Three*

DAY 1: THE GROUP ENCOUNTER

THERE'S NOTHING LIKE LOVING YOU!

Scripture Lesson: St. John 15:12

Today's Subject: LOVE AT THE NEXT LEVEL!

KEY POINTS FROM TODAY'S LESSON

Point 1

_____

_____

_____

_____

_____

_____

Point 2

_____

_____

_____

_____

_____

Point 3

_____

_____

_____

_____

_____

_____

Here's What I'm Praying For Right Now:

_____

_____

_____

_____

_____

_____

_____

_____

DAY 2: "No Limits, No Labels"

STRAIGHT FROM THE BOOK

"This is my commandment, That ye love one another, as I have loved you." (John 15:12, KJV)

JESUS SAID IT BEST

Jesus' love crossed every line: racial, social, political, economical, and spiritual. He ate with tax collectors, spoke with Samaritans, and healed Gentiles. He refused to let labels limit His love. When He said, "love one another," He meant everybody, not just people who look, live, or vote like you.

PASTOR PUTS IT LIKE THIS

Let's stop loving with fine print! For many people, who call themselves Christians, love comes with terms and conditions. It's common to hear things like, "I'll love you if you agree with me." This is not how love works in the Kingdom of our God. Jesus' love was borderless. Here is the philosophical premise we should live by and follow: if His blood covered it all, our love should reach it all. Keep this in mind, when you love without labels, you start looking like the Lord.

THINK ABOUT IT FOR A MOMENT

- Who have I labeled instead of loved?
- "Love doesn't draw lines; it builds bridges."
- Jesus loved across boundaries — and we should too.

PRAY ABOUT IT

Lord, remove the labels from my love. Help me to see people the way You do. Help me view everyone through the lens of Your grace.

In the name of Jesus, Amen!

DAY 3: "Love That Stays"

STRAIGHT FROM THE BOOK

"This is my commandment, That ye love one another, as I have loved you." (John 15:12, KJV)

JESUS SAID IT BEST

When Jesus said, "as I have loved you," He was talking about a love that stays through betrayal, denial, discomfort, dislike, problems and pain. His love didn't run when it got hard. Real love doesn't ghost people; it grows with them. Love that stays has roots, not wings. In short, the love of Jesus Christ is a love that says, "I chose to stay!"

PASTOR PUTS IT LIKE THIS

There are times when our love towards each other is like the Wi-Fi in my home. Sometimes, I have a strong signal for most of the day, but it can be gone tomorrow. However, God's love doesn't drop out. He stuck with us when we were at our worst. That's the kind of love God wants us to give others. You can't build Kingdom relationships with disposable love. Stay solid, stay steady, stay loving.

THINK ABOUT IT FOR A MOMENT

- Who in my life needs me to stay consistent in love?
- "Faithfulness is the fruit of real love."
- The same love that started should be the love that stays.

PRAY ABOUT IT

Lord, help me to be consistent in my love like You. Make me faithful, not flaky, in how I treat people.

In the name of Jesus, Amen!

DAY 4: "Love in the Trenches"

STRAIGHT FROM THE BOOK

"This is my commandment, That ye love one another, as I have loved you." (John 15:12, KJV)

JESUS SAID IT BEST

Jesus' love wasn't distant, it was love that got dirty. He touched lepers, cried with mourners, and walked with sinners. That's love in the trenches. Love that shows up when life gets messy. It's easy to love from a distance, but Jesus loved up close.

PASTOR PUTS IT LIKE THIS

Real talk for a moment today, there are some church folks that only love when the lights are on and the picture looks good. But true love shows up in the storm, not just the sunshine. Love like Jesus means being present when it's inconvenient. You can't be salt and light if you're scared to get near the dirt. This is why most churches are empty. We are large on tradition and low on love.

THINK ABOUT IT FOR A MOMENT

- Am I willing to love people in their mess, not just their miracles?
- "Love that avoids pain avoids purpose."
- Jesus didn't mind getting His hands dirty to make us clean.

PRAY ABOUT IT

Lord, help me love people where they are, not where I wish they were. Give me compassion with courage.

In the name of Jesus, Amen!

DAY 5: "Love Speaks Up"

STRAIGHT FROM THE BOOK

> "This is my commandment, That ye love one another, as I have loved you." (John 15:12, KJV)

JESUS SAID IT BEST

Jesus' love wasn't silent. He spoke the truth when it mattered, even when it was unpopular. Real love doesn't watch people walk off of a cliff, it calls them back. As you spend this devotional time with the Lord today listen to the words of Jesus with your heart, "as I have loved you." This means love with honesty and accountability.

PASTOR PUTS IT LIKE THIS

There are times that love means saying what people don't want to hear. Now here's the shout of the day, this is not being judgmental, it's being responsible. If I see you drowning and stay quiet, that's not love, that's neglect! Speak the truth, but say it with grace. That's how you love and lead like Jesus did when He walked the earth. Not long ago, I witnessed a staff member of mine tell another teammate that he was concerned about his health. The concerned staff member noticed the redness of his friend's eyes and his swollen ankles and said, "I love you too much to ignore signs like these. I'm going to help you find a good doctor because you need help." Real love speaks up!

THINK ABOUT IT FOR A MOMENT

- Who do I need to lovingly tell the truth to this week?
- "Love without truth is weak; truth without love is harsh."
- Real friends correct you in private and cover you in public.

PRAY ABOUT IT

Lord, give me the courage to speak truth in love and the wisdom to do it with grace.

In the name of Jesus, Amen!

DAY 6: "Love That Lifts"

STRAIGHT FROM THE BOOK

"This is my commandment, That ye love one another, as I have loved you." (John 15:12, KJV)

JESUS SAID IT BEST

As you read the Gospels, printed on the pages of the Bible, here's one thing that you will notice over and over again about Jesus Christ: His love lifted people! This was put on display in a literal sense. He lifted the fallen, restored the broken, enlightened the ignorant, and encouraged the weary. His love always left people better than it found them. Loving like Jesus means being a lifter.

PASTOR PUTS IT LIKE THIS

Don't be the one who drains people when they're already down. Be the one who reminds them they can still rise and run on to see what the end is going to be. You don't have to fix everybody, just lift somebody. One loving word can turn a whole day around. Lift love, because love always wins.

THINK ABOUT IT FOR A MOMENT

- Who can I lift today with a word, a call, or a smile?
- "Love lifts; pride pushes down."
- When you lift others, you lift yourself.

PRAY ABOUT IT

Lord, make me a lifter. Let my love strengthen the weak and encourage the weary.

In the name of Jesus, Amen!

DAY 7: "Love That Looks Like Jesus"

STRAIGHT FROM THE BOOK

"This is my commandment, That ye love one another, as I have loved you." (John 15:12, KJV)

JESUS SAID IT BEST

Jesus' final command wasn't about preaching or power, it was about love. The more we love like Him, the more the world sees Him through us. Love is the mirror that reflects His image. When people experience your love, they should feel like they just met a glimpse of Jesus.

PASTOR PUTS IT LIKE THIS

The great Catholic theologian, St. Francis of Assisi made a statement that I learned while in seminary that stuck with me. He said, "Preach the Gospel at all times; use words if it is completely necessary." This statement blessed me! In other words, you might be the only Bible somebody reads today, so make sure, your love is legible! When you love like Jesus, people don't just hear sermons; they see them. You can't fake the faith, it must be lived out each day of your life. Let your love preach louder than your lips. Let your walk be the talk that people want to hear.

THINK ABOUT IT FOR A MOMENT

- What does my love say about my faith?
- "Love is the loudest gospel."
- You don't need a collar to represent Christ, just compassion.

PRAY ABOUT IT

Lord, help my love to look like You. Let my actions reveal Your heart to everyone I meet.

In the name of Jesus, Amen!

CONCLUSION | WEEK *Three* | ST. JOHN 15:12

As We Conclude Week Three...

This week we explored Jesus' powerful command in St. John 15:12, where He invites us to love others with the same depth, devotion, and sacrificial commitment that He shows to us. Believers in the faith should now understand that this level of love is not optional, it is commanded, modeled, and empowered by Jesus, Himself.

This week revealed that true love flows from abiding in Christ, being transformed by His presence, and allowing His character to shape how we treat one another. Love is the fruit of abiding, the evidence of discipleship, and the heartbeat of Christian living.

WHAT WE LEARNED THIS WEEK

1. Jesus Commands Us to Love as He Loves (John 15:12)

We learned that Jesus doesn't call us to love from our own strength but from His example. His love becomes our standard and our guide.

2. Love Flows from Abiding in Christ (John 15:4–5)

This week taught us that we cannot love well apart from Jesus. As we abide in Him, His nature flows through us.

3. Love is the Visible Fruit of a Life Connected to Jesus (John 15:8)

We discovered that spiritual fruit, including love, is evidence that we belong to Christ and are walking with Him daily.

4. Christlike Love Requires Sacrifice (John 15:13)

We learned that Jesus' love is sacrificial, patient, and willing to give. Real love costs something: time, grace, patience, forgiveness.

5. Loving Others Reflects Our Friendship with Christ (John 15:14–15)

This week revealed that love is the mark of intimacy with Jesus. The more we walk with Him, the more we reflect Him.

WEEK *Three* TAKEAWAYS

- Jesus commands me to love others exactly as He has loved me.
- I cannot love well if I am not abiding well.
- Spiritual fruit is the proof of real discipleship.
- Love requires sacrifice, but Christ empowers every sacrifice I make.
- Loving others is an extension of my friendship with Jesus.
- Christlike love is patient, humble, forgiving, and consistent.
- When I love like Jesus, I reveal Him to the world around me.

WEEK *Three* FINAL PRAYER

Lord Jesus, thank You for teaching us what love truly looks like. As we conclude Week Three, help us to walk in the love You have shown us. Strengthen us to abide in You daily so that Your love flows freely through our lives. Teach us to love with patience, grace, and sacrifice. Transform our hearts so that we reflect Your character in every relationship. May our lives display Your love, and may our actions point others back to You. In Your precious name, Amen.

SECTION II - *Week Four*

DAY 1: THE GROUP ENCOUNTER

THERE'S NOTHING LIKE LOVING YOU!

Scripture Lesson: St. John 13:35

Today's Subject: CHECK OUT MY NEW LOGO!

KEY POINTS FROM TODAY'S LESSON

Point 1

_____

_____

_____

_____

_____

Point 2

_____

_____

_____

_____

_____

Point 3

_____

_____

_____

_____

_____

Here's What I'm Praying For Right Now:

_____

_____

_____

_____

_____

_____

_____

_____

DAY 2: "Recognized by Love"

STRAIGHT FROM THE BOOK

"By this shall all men know that ye are my disciples, if ye have love one to another." (John 13:35, KJV)

JESUS SAID IT BEST

Jesus Christ helped us to see what love looked like walking on two legs. He was love wrapped in a body. In other words, Jesus didn't say people would recognize His followers by miracles or money, but by mutual love. The mark of mature discipleship is love that reaches across personalities, preferences, and problems. Love is the greatest evangelistic tool there is.

PASTOR PUTS IT LIKE THIS

We live in a culture filled with people who love public recognition. It's why social media sites are so popular. There are Christian's who feel like you have to wear a huge cross and carry a Bible everywhere to represent Jesus Christ. But, if you carry love, you're already preaching! The best way to make Jesus famous is to make love visible. Be so kind that, it's confusing. Love so loud that it's unmistakable.

THINK ABOUT IT FOR A MOMENT

- Would people know I'm a disciple without me saying a word?
- "Love is louder than a sermon."
- Recognition without representation means nothing. Let love speak first.

PRAY ABOUT IT

Lord, make me recognizable by my love. Let my life silently shout that I belong to You.

In the name of Jesus, Amen!

DAY 3: "Proof of Purchase"

STRAIGHT FROM THE BOOK

"By this shall all men know that ye are my disciples, if ye have love one to another." (John 13:35, KJV)

JESUS SAID IT BEST

Jesus said love is the evidence that we've been bought with His blood. It's our "proof of purchase." When He paid the price on Calvary, He didn't just redeem us, He redefined us. Love became the receipt that shows we belong to Him.

PASTOR PUTS IT LIKE THIS

I recently purchased a really nice hoodie from an Academy Outlet. I purchased it in my normal size, but I did not try it on. When I put it on, it was just too big. I had to return it. The first thing the cashier asked me was if I had proof of purchase. Has this ever happened to you? Have you ever bought something and kept the receipt just in case? Well, God did too, and the receipt is love. When you love people, Heaven says, "paid in full." That's how the world knows who owns you. Don't hide your proof, show your receipt!

THINK ABOUT IT FOR A MOMENT

- Does my love prove I've been redeemed?
- "Love is Heaven's receipt stamped across your soul."
- Paid in full means love in full.

PRAY ABOUT IT

Lord, thank You for paying for me in love. Help me live like someone who's been purchased and purified by Your grace.

In the name of Jesus, Amen!

DAY 4: "No Love, No Credibility"

STRAIGHT FROM THE BOOK

"By this shall all men know that ye are my disciples, if ye have love one to another." (John 13:35, KJV)

JESUS SAID IT BEST

Without love, even the truth doesn't sound right. Jesus knew that a loveless faith would make the gospel unbelievable. The credibility of the Church isn't found in its buildings or budgets, it's found in believers who love like Jesus Christ.

PASTOR PUTS IT LIKE THIS

Let's be honest for a moment, the world's not leaving the Church because they don't like Jesus; they're leaving because they don't see enough of Him in us. We've got the message right but the method is wrong. Love is what gives our words weight and meaning. Without love, we just sound like noise.

THINK ABOUT IT FOR A MOMENT

- Does my love give credibility to my witness?
- "Truth without love sounds like judgment; love with truth sounds like Jesus."
- You can't win who you won't love.

PRAY ABOUT IT

Lord, don't let me preach a gospel I don't practice. Help me lead with love so people can see You through me.

In the name of Jesus, Amen!

DAY 5: "The Love Factor"

STRAIGHT FROM THE BOOK

"By this shall all men know that ye are my disciples, if ye have love one to another." (John 13:35, KJV)

JESUS SAID IT BEST

Jesus said love would be the determining factor, the "love factor". Without it, we lose our distinctiveness and meaningfulness. The "love factor" is what separates believers from the current culture: forgiving when others hold grudges, serving when others seek status, loving when others retaliate.

PASTOR PUTS IT LIKE THIS

One of my worst college subjects was Algebra. There were some of my friends that loved it, but it was a subject that gave me the blues in E flat! The thing that made Algebra difficult for me was the X factor that existed in most equations. Love is the X-factor of discipleship. It's what makes your faith look different. Anybody can clap on Sunday, but can you care on Monday? The "love factor" turns ordinary people into walking evidence of extraordinary grace.

THINK ABOUT IT FOR A MOMENT

- What's my "love factor" looking like this week?
- "Love is the difference-maker that never fails."
- The world measures success by power; Jesus measures it by love.

PRAY ABOUT IT

Lord, increase my "love factor". Let everything I do be filtered through the heart of Christ.

In the name of Jesus, Amen!

DAY 6: "Love on Display"

STRAIGHT FROM THE BOOK

"By this shall all men know that ye are my disciples, if ye have love one to another." (John 13:35, KJV)

JESUS SAID IT BEST

Jesus' command isn't just about having love, it's about showing it. Hidden love doesn't help hurting people. The love that identifies us must also be visible, practical, and public. Jesus loved out loud and He expects us to do the same.

PASTOR PUTS IT LIKE THIS

The displays on the mannequins in the mall make me want to buy what's on them every time. You see, stores want consumers, like me, to buy certain items so they simply put the items, they want you to consume on display. With this in mind, don't keep your love on private mode! Love ought to be seen in how you talk, how you forgive, how you serve. Love is a light, not a secret. Let the world see what love looks like when it wears work clothes.

THINK ABOUT IT FOR A MOMENT

- Where can I put my love on display today?
- "Love kept quiet is love cut short."
- Shine through service. That's how Jesus did it!

PRAY ABOUT IT

Lord, make my love public and powerful. Let others see You in my actions, not just my affirmations.

In the name of Jesus, Amen!

DAY 7: "Love Wins, Every Time"

STRAIGHT FROM THE BOOK

"By this shall all men know that ye are my disciples, if ye have love one to another." (John 13:35, KJV)

JESUS SAID IT BEST

Never forget this and keep it near your heart forever, if love loses, God loses because God is love. Here's the shout of knowing Jesus Christ as your personal Lord and Savior, His love in your life will never ever lose. The ultimate evidence of following Jesus is love that endures. Empires fall, trends fade, tongues fail, but love never stops winning. It's love that overcame sin, love that outlasted the grave, and love that still changes lives today!

PASTOR PUTS IT LIKE THIS

At the end of the day, when the smoke clears, the dust settles and the storm ceases, love still stands. Hate runs out of gas, but love refills itself. That's why this whole movement is about a LOVE that WINS! It's not just a tag or a title, it's a truth that endures forever. Every time we choose love, Heaven celebrates another victory!

THINK ABOUT IT FOR A MOMENT
- Where has love already won in my life?
- "Love is undefeated. The record is 1,000,000 and 0."
- The cross looked like defeat, until love got up.

PRAY ABOUT IT

Lord, thank You that Your love always wins. Help me walk daily as a living testimony of that victory.

In the name of Jesus, Amen!

CONCLUSION | WEEK FOUR | ST. JOHN 13:35

As We Conclude Week *Four*...

This week, we explored Jesus' defining statement in St. John 13:35, where He teaches that the clearest evidence of true discipleship is not knowledge, giftedness, charisma, or even spiritual discipline, it is love. Jesus reveals that authentic Christian living is measured by how we treat one another. Believers should now understand that love is the distinguishing mark of those who genuinely belong to Him.

This week revealed that loving one another is not simply an emotional expression but a spiritual demonstration. Love shows the world who we are, whose we are, and what Christ has done within us. When we choose love, we reveal the heart of God, bear witness to His transforming power, and display the unity He desires for His people.

WHAT WE LEARNED THIS WEEK

1. Love is the Evidence of True Discipleship (John 13:35)

We learned that Jesus Himself declares love to be the badge of His followers. If we truly belong to Him, love will show up in our actions, attitudes, and relationships.

2. Our Love for One Another is a Public Witness (John 13:35)

This week taught us that love is missional. The world forms its opinion of Christ based on how believers treat each other. Our unity and compassion testify about Him.

3. Christlike Love is Learned from Christ Himself (John 13:34–35)

We discovered that Jesus teaches us how to love by modeling it first. His love defines our behavior, shapes our standards, and challenges our comfort zones.

4. Love Requires Intentionality and Investment (1 John 3:18)

We learned that real love is more than words. Love is action. Love demands time, humility, forgiveness, patience, and commitment to others.

5. Loving One Another Brings God Glory (Matthew 5:16)

This week revealed that love shines the light of Christ. When we love faithfully, God is glorified, believers are strengthened, and the world sees Jesus more clearly.

WEEK *Four* TAKEAWAYS

- Love is the mark that proves I am a disciple of Jesus.
- My relationships preach a louder sermon than my words.
- Christ teaches me how to love by showing me how He loves.
- Love requires intentionality, effort, and emotional maturity.
- When I love well, God is glorified and others see Jesus in me.
- Love is action, not just emotion, speech, or sentiment.
- My willingness to love others reveals the work Christ has done in my heart.

WEEK *Four* FINAL PRAYER

Lord Jesus, thank You for teaching us that love is the true mark of discipleship. As we conclude Week Four, strengthen our hearts to love one another the way You have loved us. Help us to choose compassion over conflict, unity over division, and grace over judgment. Fill us with the power of Your Spirit so that our love becomes a witness to the world around us. Let our lives bring glory to Your name and reflect Your heart in every relationship. Shape us into disciples who are known by love. In Your precious name, Amen.

SECTION III - *Week One*

DAY 1: THE GROUP ENCOUNTER

THERE'S NOTHING LIKE LOVING GOD!

Scripture Lesson: I CAN'T STOP LOVING HIM!

Today's Subject: Psalms 116:1-2

KEY POINTS FROM TODAY'S LESSON

Point 1

_____

_____

_____

_____

_____

_____

Point 2

_____

_____

_____

_____

_____

Point 3

_____

_____

_____

_____

_____

Here's What I'm Praying For Right Now:

_____

_____

_____

_____

_____

_____

_____

_____

DAY 2: "He Heard Me"

STRAIGHT FROM THE BOOK

"I love the Lord, because he hath heard my voice and my supplications. Because he hath inclined his ear unto me, therefore will I call upon him as long as I live." (Psalm 116:1-2, KJV)

JESUS SAID IT BEST

God's Word given to us in this Psalm comes through His servant David. Here's what he said, "I love the Lord because He heard me." The word *heard* used in the passage comes from the Hebrew word *yisma*. It means to hear in the intimate sense of the term. Like a father hearing the cry of his child. This is what is expressed in today's passage. To hear in this regard is love rooted in relationship, not religion. God doesn't just hear prayers, He hears His children. When you cry out in pain, when you whisper in fear, when you shout in joy, the Lord our God doesn't just hear every word, He hears every syllable! That's why loving God begins with gratitude for His listening ear.

PASTOR PUTS IT LIKE THIS

If you've ever prayed and God actually answered, you know what David's talking about! Here's the shout of the day. God heard you when others ignored you. He caught tears nobody saw. That's why we love Him, not just for miracles, but for moments like these. He heard us when we weren't even sure what to say or how to say it.

THINK ABOUT IT FOR A MOMENT

- What has God heard from me lately: worship or worry?
- "God's ear is never out of range."
- God hears the silent as well as the audible.

PRAY ABOUT IT

Lord, thank You for hearing me, even when I didn't know how to talk to You right. You always listen, and for that I love You.

In the name of Jesus, Amen!

DAY 3: "Call Waiting"

STRAIGHT FROM THE BOOK

"I love the Lord, because he hath heard my voice and my supplications. Because he hath inclined his ear unto me, therefore will I call upon him as long as I live." (Psalm 116:1-2, KJV)

JESUS SAID IT BEST

One of the most interesting facets of this passage is the word *inclined*. David says God *inclined* His ear, meaning one of three things or perhaps all of them occurred at once. God looked in your direction, He leaned towards you when you started to pray, and He listened intently to what you had to say. Here's the radical truth of the matter, God isn't distant. He's ever present and attentive! Every time you pray, Heaven leans forward. Jesus modeled that intimacy with the Father. He prayed like someone who knew God was listening. That's a love that is life-changing.

PASTOR PUTS IT LIKE THIS

I talk for a living. I'm either preaching, teaching, speaking, conversing or just plain ole talking. Be honest, have you ever tried talking to someone who's half-listening? Isn't it just the worst thing ever? They're scrolling while you're sharing. They're nodding and yawning while you are speaking. Here's the shout of the day, that ain't God! When you call Him, He leans in. He listens carefully and His line never drops.

THINK ABOUT IT FOR A MOMENT

- How often do I call God just to say, "I love You"?
- "Prayer isn't duty, it's dialogue."
- God's got you on His speed dial of grace.

PRAY ABOUT IT

Lord, thank You for always leaning in to hear me. Help me call on You out of love, not just need.

In the name of Jesus, Amen!

DAY 4: "Reasons Why I Love Him"

STRAIGHT FROM THE BOOK

"I love the Lord, because he hath heard my voice and my supplications. Because he hath inclined his ear unto me, therefore will I call upon him as long as I live." (Psalm 116:1-2, KJV)

JESUS SAID IT BEST

Loving God means remembering why you love Him. David's "because" matters. It's gratitude in motion. God's goodness deserves acknowledgment. Jesus taught that the one who's forgiven much loves much. Love grows deeper when we count the reasons for it.

PASTOR PUTS IT LIKE THIS

Take a moment to survey the landscape of your own soul. Consider some of the things that God has done for you, that He just did not have to do. Do thoughts of what the Lord has done and provided for you bring you to the point that your "thank You" turns into a shout? That's the "because" factor! He healed me, that's one. He kept me, that's two. He forgave me, that's three. Before you know it, you've got a praise list that's longer than any list of problems you could have ever possibly produced.

THINK ABOUT IT FOR A MOMENT

- What's one reason I can give God thanks for today?
- "Your 'because' builds your belief."
- When you forget why, your worship gets weak.

PRAY ABOUT IT

Lord, thank You for every reason You've given me to love You. I'll spend my life saying, "because You're good."

In the name of Jesus, Amen!

DAY 5: "Love on the Line"

STRAIGHT FROM THE BOOK

"I love the Lord, because he hath heard my voice and my supplications. Because he hath inclined his ear unto me, therefore will I call upon him as long as I live." (Psalm 116:1-2, KJV)

JESUS SAID IT BEST

Prayer is the line that keeps love alive. When you love someone, you talk to them, not just when you're in trouble, but because healthy relational constructs bring comfort and consolation. In our study passage this week, given from the Word of the Lord, comes a promise. Here's what it says, "….I will call upon Him as long as I live." This says I will love the Lord forever, no matter what!

PASTOR PUTS IT LIKE THIS

Phone plans can be frustrating to negotiate to say the least. It doesn't matter whether it's T-Mobile, Verizon or Spectrum. However, imagine for a moment, that prayer was a phone plan! Some of us would've been cut off long ago for dropped calls, none payment and no usage! But thank God for unlimited minutes, no dropped calls and bills paid on auto-pay from His account! Here's the shout, God never puts you on hold. So talk to Him, not just when it hurts, but when it's good. Keep your "love line" open.

THINK ABOUT IT FOR A MOMENT

- How's my communication with God lately?
- "Love dies when communication dries."
- Keep your prayer line connected, that's where the power flows.

PRAY ABOUT IT

Lord, thank You for never hanging up on me. Teach me to stay connected through prayer and praise every day.

In the name of Jesus, Amen!

DAY 6: "Love That Listens Back"

STRAIGHT FROM THE BOOK

"I love the Lord, because he hath heard my voice and my supplications. Because he hath inclined his ear unto me, therefore will I call upon him as long as I live." (Psalm 116:1-2, KJV)

JESUS SAID IT BEST

Jesus isn't just a Shepherd that loves His flock as He leads them. He listens too! With this in mind, love isn't a one-way street of communication. God listens to us, but He also wants us to listen to Him. Jesus said, "my sheep hear My voice." In other words, love deepens through dialogue. When you slow down long enough to hear God's whisper, you start living in step with an inner voice that speaks softly to your soul regarding His will for your life.

PASTOR PUTS IT LIKE THIS

It's very frustrating to talk to someone and they do all of the talking. In this stead, you can't say you love God and always do the talking! Sometimes you've got to hush your mouth and open your heart. God's trying to drop direction in your spirit, but He can't get a word in! Prayer ain't just speaking, it's hearing. Listen for the love in His instructions.

THINK ABOUT IT FOR A MOMENT

- Do I listen when God speaks, or just speak when I need Him?
- "The quiet place is where love grows loud."
- Hearing God is proof of knowing Him.

PRAY ABOUT IT

Lord, speak to me. Help me to listen with love and obey with joy.

In the name of Jesus, Amen!

DAY 7: "As Long As I Live"

STRAIGHT FROM THE BOOK

"I love the Lord, because he hath heard my voice and my supplications. Because he hath inclined his ear unto me, therefore will I call upon him as long as I live." (Psalm 116:1-2, KJV)

JESUS SAID IT BEST

Notice the last five words of our study passage. It gives us David's love language of longevity and perpetuity. He says, "as long as I live." Jesus called for that same kind of endurance when He said, "abide in Me." Loving God isn't seasonal; it's steadfast. Real love doesn't retire, it remains. It doesn't pause, it persists.

PASTOR PUTS IT LIKE THIS

My college days were filled with "on-again, off-again" relationships. I really like her, but she won't act right. She likes me, but she just isn't right. Have you ever been there before? "On-again, off-again" relationships can be worrisome, time consuming and terribly frustrating. If we'd be honest, we've all had "on-again, off-again" relationships, but God ain't one of them. He's on all of the time without fail. It's why we love Him for life! Keep showing up for Him the way He keeps showing up for you. This love story doesn't fade, it's built on a faith that will never ever fail!

THINK ABOUT IT FOR A MOMENT

- How consistent is my love for God?
- "Real love lasts longer than feelings."
- I don't just love Him for a moment, I love Him for life.

PRAY ABOUT IT

Lord, may my love for You never fade. From my first breath to my last, I'll keep calling on Your name.

In the name of Jesus, Amen!

CONCLUSION | WEEK ONE | PSALM 116:1–2

As We Conclude Week *One*...

This week, we entered a powerful new section of study by reflecting on the psalmist's heartfelt declaration in Psalm 116:1–2. Believers in the faith should now understand that love for God is not abstract or theoretical, but it is personal, experiential, and rooted in God's attentive grace towards all of His children.

This week revealed that our love for the Lord flows from His love for us. He hears us when we cry. He bends down to listen when we pray. He responds with compassion, mercy, and comfort. Because God listens with intention and leans toward us with divine care, we are compelled to trust Him, to call on Him, and to walk with Him throughout our lives.

WHAT WE LEARNED THIS WEEK

1. God Hears Our Cry (Psalm 116:1)

We learned that one of the greatest assurances of faith is this: God hears us even if our cry is silent. He is not distant, distracted, or disengaged. Our prayers matter to the Lord.

2. God Inclines His Ear Toward Us (Psalm 116:2)

This week taught us that God doesn't merely listen, He leans in. The image of God inclining His ear reveals His nearness, His tenderness, and His desire for relationship.

3. Love for God is a Response to His Faithfulness (Psalm 116:1)

We discovered that the psalmist's love is anchored in experience. Because God has heard, helped, delivered, and sustained him, his heart overflows with love and devotion.

4. Prayer Is a Lifelong Commitment (Psalm 116:2)

We learned that because God is faithful, we should be faithful. The psalmist declares that he will call upon the Lord "as long as I live," teaching us that prayer is not seasonal. Prayer is a lifestyle.

5. God's Attentiveness Builds Our Confidence (Psalm 34:15)

This week revealed that when we know God is listening, we pray with boldness, live with peace, and trust Him more deeply in every circumstance.

WEEK *One* TAKEAWAYS

- God hears my voice and cares about what concerns me.
- The Lord inclines His ear toward me. He listens with love.
- My love for God grows out of my experience with His faithfulness.
- Prayer is not optional; it is a lifelong conversation with God.
- God's attentiveness gives me confidence to call on Him in every season.
- When God listens, He responds. His responses are always righteous and gracious.
- My relationship with God is strengthened each time I cry out to Him.

WEEK *One* FINAL PRAYER

Father, thank You for being a God who hears. As we conclude Week One of Section III, remind us daily that You listen to our cries, our concerns, and our quiet prayers. Help us to grow in love and devotion because of Your faithfulness. Teach us to call upon You with confidence, to trust Your responses, and to walk with You throughout our lives. May our hearts overflow with gratitude for Your nearness, and may our prayers rise to You with sincerity and expectation. In Jesus' name, Amen.

SECTION III - *Week Two*

DAY 1: The Group Encounter

THERE'S NOTHING LIKE LOVING GOD!

Scripture Lesson: 1 John 4:19

Today's Subject: He's Loving It Out Of Us!

KEY POINTS FROM TODAY'S LESSON

Point 1

_____

_____

_____

_____

_____

Point 2

_____

_____

_____

_____

_____

Point 3

_____

_____

_____

_____

_____

_____

_____

Here's What I'm Praying For Right Now:

_____

_____

_____

_____

_____

_____

_____

_____

DAY 2: "Love Started It"

STRAIGHT FROM THE BOOK

"We love him, because he first loved us." (1 John 4:19, KJV)

JESUS SAID IT BEST

This may be difficult for some to fully understand, but it is true none-the-less. Here is what the grip of God's grace is rooted in, before you ever said, "Lord, I love You," He had already said, "I love you first." God made up His mind about you before the earth had an axis to spin on or the moon had a glow. Before you were conceived or thought about, God decided to love you. This reality is the foundation of every believer's faith. God's love was proactive, not reactive. Jesus proved it on the cross, loving us while we were still lost, still stubborn, still stuck and still trapped in sin. Love didn't start with a choir; it started with a cross.

PASTOR PUTS IT LIKE THIS

Like a Netflix Series, the Bible is one big love story. You are the object and God is the subject! The celebration of this radical truth begins with the fact that you didn't start this love story, God did! He showed up first, before you prayed, before you preached, before you even believed. That's why we don't have to earn His love; we just return it. He made the first move, and it was permanent.

THINK ABOUT IT FOR A MOMENT

- What does it mean that God "started it"?
- "Grace moved first."
- When you realize He loved you first, you stop trying to prove your worth.

PRAY ABOUT IT

Lord, thank You for loving me before I ever looked for You. Teach me to respond to Your first love with lasting devotion.

In the name of Jesus, Amen!

DAY 3: "All Natural, No Preservatives"

STRAIGHT FROM THE BOOK

"We love him, because he first loved us." (1 John 4:19, KJV)

JESUS SAID IT BEST

All too often, we think that we can earn God's love or cause Him to love us for some good deed performed or some holy action that makes Him really like us. But, God's Word is clear, His love wasn't triggered by our goodness; it was born from His nature; therefore, it was all natural. Scripture teaches us that "God is love." No additives, no preservatives. It was pure love. "First love" means unprovoked love. In short, it's love that didn't wait for you to deserve it. Jesus washed feet before anyone asked, forgave before anyone apologized, and gave before anyone believed.

PASTOR PUTS IT LIKE THIS

Religious people have a very difficult time comprehending this reality; however, once you come to grips with it, your life changes forever! You didn't do anything to make God love you, and you can't do anything to make Him stop. His love is self-starting and self-sustaining. It doesn't need a reason; it is the reason! That's the kind of love that'll have you shouting while you sit at a red light in traffic! He loves you!

THINK ABOUT IT FOR A MOMENT

- How does it feel knowing His love isn't performance-based?
- "You can't out-sin a love that started before sin."

- His love runs on mercy, not on merit.
  ### *PRAY ABOUT IT*

Lord, thank You for loving me for no reason other than that You are love. Keep me amazed by Your unprovoked grace.

In the name of Jesus, Amen!

DAY 4: "You Can't Sin Love Away"

STRAIGHT FROM THE BOOK

"We love him, because he first loved us." (1 John 4:19, KJV)

JESUS SAID IT BEST

God's love is not passive, it pursues. Jesus said He came to "seek and to save that which was lost" (St. Luke 19:10). Divine love doesn't wait for you to find it; it hunts you down with mercy. Every detour you took, love followed. Every wrong turn, grace rerouted.

PASTOR PUTS IT LIKE THIS

Years ago while frustrated with Christianity, I did my best to "sin" God away. I did it wrong and did not want to get it right. Have you ever been there before, where you did what you wanted to do without repentance? Here's the shout of the day, you discovered God would chase you down with His love! You picked a bottle and love was right there. You decided not to go to church and love was still right there. You were ducking, dodging, and drifting, but love still found you. It showed up in second chances, in unexpected peace, in midnight mercy. That's why you can't outrun His goodness, He's faster than your failures and more faithful than your foolishness!

THINK ABOUT IT FOR A MOMENT
- Where has God's love "caught" me lately?
- "Grace doesn't give up easily."
- If love is chasing you right now, stop running and let love win.

PRAY ABOUT IT

Lord, thank You for chasing me when I didn't even want to be found. Help me slow down and stay caught by Your love.

In the name of Jesus, Amen!

DAY 5: "The Love That Took Me to a Whole Different Level"

STRAIGHT FROM THE BOOK

"We love him, because he first loved us." (1 John 4:19, KJV)

JESUS SAID IT BEST

The love of God doesn't just reach, it raises. Every time Jesus encountered brokenness, He lifted people higher. The woman at the well (St. John 4), the man on the mat (St. John 5), the woman with the issue of the blood (St. Mark 5:34-43) and the thief on the cross (St. Luke 23:42-43). Love met them low and left them lifted high!

PASTOR PUTS IT LIKE THIS

I used to love going shopping with my grandmother, Big Momma. She would go to Sears and Roebuck and she would enter at the bottom floor and take the elevator up to every level before we would leave the store. The bottom floor would have lawnmowers and yard rakes. But, the top floor would be filled with fine china and gorgeous lamps. That's how God's love is. It takes you to different levels and each level gets greater! That old hymn said it right: "love lifted me!" Here's the shout of the day, you didn't climb out, love pulled you out. Your guilt tried to drown you, but grace showed up and grabbed you! Every breath you breathe now is love's reminder that you made it up and out.

THINK ABOUT IT FOR A MOMENT

- What did God's love lift me out of?
- "If it wasn't for love, I'd still be stuck."
- The higher you go, the more grateful you should be.

PRAY ABOUT IT

Lord, thank You for lifting me when I couldn't lift myself. Keep me standing strong in the arms that raised me.

In the name of Jesus, Amen!

DAY 6: "Love That Lasts"

STRAIGHT FROM THE BOOK

"We love him, because he first loved us." (1 John 4:19, KJV)

JESUS SAID IT BEST

God's love doesn't expire. The same love that saved you still sustains you. Jesus said, "Lo, I am with you always." His presence is proof of His permanence. When people change, when life shifts, His love stays solid.

PASTOR PUTS IT LIKE THIS

Hey, did you know that canned goods have expiration dates attached to them? We all know that milk has a pull date. But, canned goods have one too. I was working with a dear friend of mine and discovered that canned goods do not last always. Expiration dates remind us all that things were not meant to last forever. Fads fade, feelings flip, but God's love never ever changes. You can hang your hope on that. People may unfollow you, but God's love is still subscribed. His notifications never turn off. When everything else runs out, love remains forever.

THINK ABOUT IT FOR A MOMENT

- How has God's love stayed constant in my chaos?
- "Eternal means everyday."
- Love that lasts keeps you from losing heart.

PRAY ABOUT IT

Lord, I'm grateful that Your love never gives up, never grows old, and never goes away. Keep me steady in Your everlasting arms.

In the name of Jesus, Amen!

DAY 7: "I Clapped Back"

STRAIGHT FROM THE BOOK

"We love him, because he first loved us." (1 John 4:19, KJV)

JESUS SAID IT BEST

Never forget this very important principle, our love for God is a response to His love for us. With this in mind, our love is not forced; it's a reflex. When you truly realize how deeply He loves you, worship becomes automatic. Gratitude kicks in like muscle memory. You don't think about it, you just love Him back.

PASTOR PUTS IT LIKE THIS

My mother kept hot pots on the kitchen stove. If you ever touched one that was still hot without a towel or a kitchen glove on your hand, it would be a natural reflex to snatch your hand back. That's a reflex. Well, when God blesses you, a "thank You, Lord" ought to leap from your lungs the exact same way! When you remember His mercy, a public praise should come from your soul on its own. By the way, reflex love doesn't wait for Sunday morning during worship; it responds in real time. If the Lord has loved and blessed you in some real ways, start your day by saying "I clapped back!"

THINK ABOUT IT FOR A MOMENT

- What triggers my reflex of worship?
- "Grateful hearts react fast."
- Love that's real always responds.

PRAY ABOUT IT

Lord, keep my heart sensitive to Your goodness. Let every reminder of Your love trigger an immediate response of worship.

In the name of Jesus, Amen!

CONCLUSION | WEEK TWO | 1 JOHN 4:19

As We Conclude Week *Two...*

This week, we reflected deeply on the powerful truth found in 1 John 4:19, where the Apostle John reveals the foundation of all Christian love: God loved us first. Believers in the faith should now understand that our love for God is not initiated by human effort, emotional strength, or spiritual maturity. It begins with God's sovereign, unconditional, and eternal love poured out on us.

This week revealed that everything we do as believers: loving God, loving others, and even loving ourselves, is a response to the love God has already demonstrated. Before we prayed, He loved us. Before we believed, He loved us. Before we stopped lying, smoking, stealing, cheating, drinking, or gambling, He loved us. Before we changed, repented, or grew, He loved us. His love is the origin, the motivation, and the sustaining power behind our spiritual lives.

WHAT WE LEARNED THIS WEEK

1. God Loved Us First (1 John 4:19)

We learned that divine love did not start with us, it started in the heart of God. His love precedes us, pursues us, and surrounds us.

2. Our Love for God is a Response, Not an Initiation (1 John 4:19)

This week taught us that we do not initiate love toward God; we respond to the love He has already shown. Our devotion is fueled by His faithfulness.

3. God's Love is Unconditional and Unchanging (Jeremiah 31:3)

We discovered that God's love is everlasting. It is not based on performance, perfection, or personality. It is based on His nature.

4. Real Love Flows From Experiencing God's Love Personally (1 John 4:16)

We learned that when we abide in the love of God, we are empowered to love others, forgive deeply, and walk in spiritual confidence.

5. God's Love Transforms Our Identity (Romans 5:8)

This week revealed that knowing God loved us at our worst gives us courage, acceptance, and freedom in Christ. His love changes how we see Him and how we see ourselves.

WEEK *Two* TAKEAWAYS

- God loved me before I ever knew Him.
- My love for God is fueled by His love for me.
- God's love is unconditional, eternal, and unchanging.
- Experiencing God's love transforms my ability to love others.
- I am free to love boldly because I am fully loved by God.
- God's love shapes my identity, my confidence, and my purpose.
- The more I meditate on God's love, the stronger my devotion becomes.

WEEK *Two* FINAL PRAYER

Father, thank You for loving us first. As we conclude Week Two of Section III, remind us daily that Your love is the foundation of our faith. Help us to rest in the truth that Your love preceded our decisions, our growth, and our commitment. Teach us to walk confidently in Your love and to respond with gratitude, obedience, and devotion. Let Your love flow through every area of our lives so that we may reflect You clearly to others. Thank You for loving us unconditionally and eternally. In Jesus' name, Amen.

SECTION III - *Week Three*

DAY 1: THE GROUP ENCOUNTER

THERE'S NOTHING LIKE LOVING GOD!

Scripture Lesson: Deuteronomy 6:5

Today's Subject: I'm Real With It!

KEY POINTS FROM TODAY'S LESSON

Point 1

_____

_____

_____

_____

_____

_____

Point 2

_____

_____

_____

_____

_____

Point 3

_____

_____

_____

_____

_____

_____

Here's What I'm Praying For Right Now:

_____

_____

_____

_____

_____

_____

_____

_____

_____

DAY 2: "I'm All In"

STRAIGHT FROM THE BOOK

"And thou shalt love the Lord thy God with all thine heart, and with all thy soul, and with all thy might." (Deuteronomy 6:5, KJV)

JESUS SAID IT BEST

This verse doesn't stand alone. It is connected to verse 4 and is the most quoted verse in all of the Old Testament. It is called the *Shema*. It calls Israel to hear in the sense that they are obligated to pay close attention to what is to follow and verse 5 quoted above is what follows. With this in mind, this passage isn't about casual affection, but about complete devotion. God doesn't ask for some of your heart; He wants all of it. Jesus repeated these words when He was asked what the greatest commandment was. Loving God with everything you are: your heart, soul, mind, and strength. This means He's not just a priority; He is the priority.

PASTOR PUTS IT LIKE THIS

There are times when we treat God like He's taking applications for part-time lovers. However, the truth of the matter is that He's looking for full-time faithful followers! "All in" means you don't keep God on a time clock. He's the whole schedule. When you give Him your heart, He'll handle your hustle. Stop holding back the best of you and give Him the rest of you. Go all in because He's worth it!

THINK ABOUT IT FOR A MOMENT

- What would "all in" love for God look like in my life?
- "Half-hearted love produces half-lived faith."
- Love God like there's no backup plan.

PRAY ABOUT IT

Lord, take all of me! Take my heart, my habits, my hopes. I want to love You without any limits.

In the name of Jesus, Amen!

DAY 3: "Heart Work"

STRAIGHT FROM THE BOOK

> **"And thou shalt love the Lord thy God with all thine heart, and with all thy soul, and with all thy might." (Deuteronomy 6:5, KJV)**

JESUS SAID IT BEST

Loving God starts in the heart. The Hebrew word for *heart* means the place where desires, motives, and emotions live. Jesus said, "where your treasure is, there will your heart be also." Here's the central idea presented in our study passage for the week, real love for God begins when you treasure Him above everything else.

PASTOR PUTS IT LIKE THIS

In the sport of baseball, the heart of the game is found at home plate. Everything else that takes place is attached to this one plate. A runner only scores if he can reach home plate. The pitcher has to throw the ball over home plate. Thus, the heart of the game is the place the game calls home. With this in mind, your heart is God's home base. But let's be honest, sometimes we try to keep Him on the bases and we never bring Him in! Loving God with all your heart means letting Him move in, not just visit. It's heart work, not hard work. When He's got your heart, obedience becomes natural. He becomes the center of everything that you do and believe.

THINK ABOUT IT FOR A MOMENT

- What's taking up too much space in my heart?
- "A cluttered heart can't carry full love."
- Give God the keys to your heart and not just weekend access-pass to your emotions.

PRAY ABOUT IT

Lord, clean my heart and fill it with love for You. Take up full residence inside me.

In the name of Jesus, Amen!

DAY 4: "Every Part of Me"

STRAIGHT FROM THE BOOK

"And thou shalt love the Lord thy God with all thine heart, and with all thy soul, and with all thy might." (Deuteronomy 6:5, KJV)

JESUS SAID IT BEST

When we see the word *soul* in the Bible, we think of it in Greek or Western terms. This means that we see the soul as something that cannot be touched with human hands. However, the Hebrew notion of *soul (Nephesh)* is totally different. It means every part of your human existence. Therefore, to love God with your soul means to love Him with your head, hands, feet, arms, legs, lungs, vocal chords, every part of your body. Jesus said, "My soul is exceedingly sorrowful," yet He still said, "not my will, but Yours be done." He knew that the cross would cost Him everything and did it anyway.

PASTOR PUTS IT LIKE THIS

Love from your soul love hits different! Love from your soul says "Lord, I love you" when it hurts, when you don't understand, when you have more question marks than you do exclamation marks. It's a love that says, "nevertheless and despite everything" my soul says I love you. That's grown-up faith. That's love that survives every storm and every moment of adversity.

THINK ABOUT IT FOR A MOMENT

- Does my soul still say "yes" when life says "no"?
- "Soul love is surrender love."
- Sometimes loving God means trusting Him blind.

PRAY ABOUT IT

Lord, I love You with my soul, through both sorrow and success. Help me trust You even when I can't trace You.

In the name of Jesus, Amen!

DAY 5: "Love That's Strong"

STRAIGHT FROM THE BOOK

"And thou shalt love the Lord thy God with all thine heart, and with all thy soul, and with all thy might." (Deuteronomy 6:5, KJV)

JESUS SAID IT BEST

God deserves love strong and solid and not love that is weak and flimsy. Jesus served until He sweated blood. That's love that gives its last and still glorifies God. To love with all your might means giving God all of your effort, energy, excellence and endurance.

PASTOR PUTS IT LIKE THIS

People hustle for what they value and appreciate. However, when it comes to expressing that same passion towards the Lord, we give God what we have left and not what's right. We hustle at work and give God very little when it comes to commitment. We are often fired up for our favorite team to play but lose that same enthusiasm when it comes to worship in the corporate setting. In short, some of us just don't worship fired up. We worship like we are tired. God's been too good for lazy love! If you can shout at the game, you can praise the Lord our God in church! Give Him that strong love! The kind of love that shows up early, stays late, and keeps the fire burning.

THINK ABOUT IT FOR A MOMENT

- Where do I need to strengthen my love for God?
- "Tired love won't carry you through tough times."
- Love is proven by effort, not emotion.

PRAY ABOUT IT

Lord, renew my strength so I can serve You with excellence. Let my energy match my gratitude.

In the name of Jesus, Amen!

DAY 6: "It's Gonna Cost You Something"

STRAIGHT FROM THE BOOK

"And thou shalt love the Lord thy God with all thine heart, and with all thy soul, and with all thy might." (Deuteronomy 6:5, KJV)

JESUS SAID IT BEST

Real love is never cheap. Jesus said, "greater love hath no man than this, that a man lay down his life for his friends" (St. John 15:13, KJV). Loving God with all you are will cost something: your comfort, control, and convenience. Love that costs nothing is worth nothing. But when love costs you everything(,) it's because what you love is worth everything to you.

PASTOR PUTS IT LIKE THIS

Don't judge me, but I love online shopping. Sometimes the bargains can be incredible! Not long ago, I found some Christian Louboutin's men's loafers for only $99.95! I jumped on my deal right away. However, when they arrived, I realized they were cheap knock-off's. My feelings were crushed. I made my way to the Louboutin shop in the Houston Galleria and asked the salesman when do these shoes go on sale. He smirked and said, "never! When you buy Christian Louboutin it's going to cost you something." People were buying them like crazy because they loved them! Here's what I think, if people can buy shoes at full price because they love them, it stands to reason that we can love God with everything in us because we love Him! Remember this, it's gonna cost you something!

THINK ABOUT IT FOR A MOMENT

- What has loving God cost me, and what has it given me?
- "If love doesn't stretch you, it won't strengthen you."
- Sacrifice is love's proof of purchase.

PRAY ABOUT IT

Lord, I know love costs, but I'm willing to pay the price. You gave me everything, so I'll hold nothing back.

In the name of Jesus, Amen!

DAY 7: "The One I Really Love"

STRAIGHT FROM THE BOOK

"And thou shalt love the Lord thy God with all thine heart, and with all thy soul, and with all thy might." (Deuteronomy 6:5, KJV)

JESUS SAID IT BEST

Jesus reminded us, "you cannot serve two masters." Loving God with all your being means staying focused, not distracted by idols, opportunities, and insecurities. Here's the bottom line to the love found in our scripture lesson for the week: single-minded love produces supernatural peace.

PASTOR PUTS IT LIKE THIS

The devil is a master deceiver. He loves pushing distractions your way so that he can divide your devotion! Keep this in mind, the devil doesn't have to destroy you if he can just distract you. Keep your eyes on the One who never took His eyes off you! When you make God the one you really love, your love for Him will put your life in order. The end result is a freedom that no one else can give you but Him!

THINK ABOUT IT FOR A MOMENT

- What's been competing for my love lately?
- "Divided love leads to distracted living."
- Stay fixed on the One who first fixed you.

PRAY ABOUT IT

Lord, refocus my heart on You. Help me remove anything that's stealing my attention or affection.

In the name of Jesus, Amen!

CONCLUSION | WEEK THREE | DEUTERONOMY 6:5

As We Conclude Week *Three*...

This week, we explored the foundational command of Deuteronomy 6:5, one of the most essential verses in all of Scripture. Believers in the faith should now understand that loving God is not a suggestion, an emotional feeling, or a seasonal response. It is a divine command that calls for total devotion.

This week revealed that loving God with all our heart, soul, and might encompasses every part of who we are. It is a love that involves our emotions, our decisions, our inner life, our physical energy, and our daily actions. God is not interested in partial affection or divided loyalties. He desires and deserves our whole selves, every thought we think, every breath we breathe, every gift we possess, and every step we take.

WHAT WE LEARNED THIS WEEK

1. Loving God Requires Our Whole Heart (Deuteronomy 6:5)

We learned that true love for God begins internally. The heart represents our affections, desires, motives, and intentions. God wants love that is sincere, undivided, and authentic.

2. Loving God Involves Our Soul (Deuteronomy 6:5)

This week taught us that the soul includes our mind, our will, and our emotional life. Loving God means surrendering our thoughts, aligning our decisions, and trusting Him with our deep places.

3. Loving God With Our Might Means Loving Him With Our Strength (Deuteronomy 6:5)

We discovered that "might" refers to energy, resources, ability, and effort. Loving God means not giving Him our leftovers, but giving Him our best, our strength and our commitment.

4. Loving God Requires Daily Intentionality (Joshua 22:5)

We learned that wholehearted love is not accidental. It grows through obedience, worship, prayer, and consistent pursuit of God.

5. Loving God Shapes Every Area of Life (Matthew 22:37)

This week revealed that Jesus affirms Deuteronomy 6:5 as the greatest commandment. Love for God influences our relationships, decisions, priorities, and purpose.

WEEK *Three* TAKEAWAYS

- God desires love that involves every part of who I am.
- Loving God with my whole heart means giving Him sincere and undivided affection.
- Loving God with my soul means surrendering my thoughts, will, and emotions to Him.
- Loving God with my might means giving Him my strength, energy, and resources.
- Love for God must be intentional, consistent, and cultivated daily.
- Jesus confirms that loving God completely is the foundation of spiritual life.
- When I love God fully, everything in my life comes into divine alignment.

WEEK *Three* FINAL PRAYER

Father, thank You for calling us to love You with all our heart, soul, and might. As we conclude Week Three of Section III, help us to grow into a deeper, more intentional love for You. Teach us to give You our whole heart without reservation, our whole soul without hesitation, and our full strength without withholding anything. Align our desires with Your will, shape our thoughts with Your truth, and strengthen our lives by Your presence. May our love for You be evident in how we live, serve, worship, and obey. In Jesus' name, Amen.

SECTION III - *Week Four*

DAY 1: THE GROUP ENCOUNTER

THERE'S NOTHING LIKE LOVING GOD!

Scripture Lesson: 1 John 4:20

Today's Subject: Be Careful It's A Two-Way Street!

KEY POINTS FROM TODAY'S LESSON

Point 1

_____

_____

_____

_____

_____

Point 2

_____

_____

_____

_____

_____

Point 3

_____

_____

_____

_____

_____

_____

_____

Here's What I'm Praying For Right Now:

_____

_____

_____

_____

_____

_____

_____

_____

DAY 2: "Love Don't Lie"

STRAIGHT FROM THE BOOK

If a man say, I love God, and hateth his brother, he is a liar: for he that loveth not his brother whom he hath seen, how can he love God whom he hath not seen?

(1 John 4:20, KJV)

JESUS SAID IT BEST

This is one of the most piercing, powerful and provocative verses in the Bible. The Disciple John makes the argument that it is impossible to love Jesus and hate your brother. The term *hate*, used in the passage, comes from a term that means to not just be the opposite of love, but the absence of it. Jesus said, "by this shall all men know that ye are my disciples, if ye have love one to another." With this in mind, real love tells the truth and the truth is, you can't love God and hate people at the same time. Love and hate can't share the same heart.

PASTOR PUTS IT LIKE THIS

Not long ago while driving east bound on the I-10 corridor near my home, I witnessed something that just floored me. I saw a red sedan that had a huge "honk if you love Jesus" bumper sticker on their car, all the while, trying to run another car off of the road. Get this, some people love God, but have road rage in their hearts for the people who God created. Here's what God is saying, don't just talk love, live it. In other words, real love don't lie! If you say you love Him, it'll show up in how you treat them. That's not hypocrisy, that's holiness.

THINK ABOUT IT FOR A MOMENT

- Is my love for people telling the truth about my love for God?
- Real love is always visible.

PRAY ABOUT IT

Lord, don't let me say I love You while acting like I don't. Make my love consistent, clean, and credible.

In the name of Jesus, Amen!

DAY 3: "Love You Can See"

STRAIGHT FROM THE BOOK

If a man say, I love God, and hateth his brother, he is a liar: for he that loveth not his brother whom he hath seen, how can he love God whom he hath not seen?

(1 John 4:20, KJV)

JESUS SAID IT BEST

Jesus told us to love our neighbour as ourselves. John takes it deeper. Love you can't see is proven by love that can be seen. How we handle people reveals how we honor God. How we handle them is a direct reflection of how we feel about Him. When love goes invisible, faith becomes unbelievable. But, when God's love is visible, our faith in the Lord Jesus Christ becomes touchable and tangible. In short, it becomes love you can see!

PASTOR PUTS IT LIKE THIS

At the Antioch church, where I'm privileged to be commissioned by the Lord to serve as Pastor, I share this one sentiment each week with our congregation. I tell them, "don't tell me you love God if you can't even speak to your neighbor standing right next to you." Love you can see looks like kindness, forgiveness, and compassion. God is invisible, but people are not! With this in mind, how you treat them shows who's really ruling your heart.

THINK ABOUT IT FOR A MOMENT
- Who around me needs to see God's love through me?
- "Invisible love isn't believable love."
- If they can't see your God, they should still feel your grace.

PRAY ABOUT IT

Lord, help me to love visibly and tangibly. Let my actions make You easy to recognize.

In the name of Jesus, Amen!

DAY 4: "Check Your Heart"

STRAIGHT FROM THE BOOK

If a man say, I love God, and hateth his brother, he is a liar: for he that loveth not his brother whom he hath seen, how can he love God whom he hath not seen?

(1 John 4:20, KJV)

JESUS SAID IT BEST

Jesus warned that the heart reveals the truth: "Out of the abundance of the heart, the mouth speaketh." John challenges believers to check their hearts, not just their hands. Love isn't a performance; it's a posture of the heart that reflects Heaven's rhythm.

PASTOR PUTS IT LIKE THIS

I was raised by a Pastor-Daddy who hailed from the big city of Melville, Louisiana. Even though he now rests with the ancestors, his legacy of preaching and teaching lives in my heart. In one of his sermons he said, "you can't fake love forever. Sooner or later, your heart will tell on you!" Ask God for a love checkup. Ask Him in prayer, "Lord, is there hate hiding in me?" Sometimes unforgiveness is just hate wearing a church outfit. Get rid of it! You can't carry healing and hostility in the same heart.

THINK ABOUT IT FOR A MOMENT

- What's in my heart that blocks love from flowing freely?
- "Heart maintenance is holiness maintenance."
- Love flows best through a clean heart.

PRAY ABOUT IT

Lord, search my heart. Remove any bitterness or hate that keeps love from flowing.

In the name of Jesus, Amen!

DAY 5: "Vertical and Horizontal"

STRAIGHT FROM THE BOOK

If a man say, I love God, and hateth his brother, he is a liar: for he that loveth not his brother whom he hath seen, how can he love God whom he hath not seen?

(1 John 4:20, KJV)

JESUS SAID IT BEST

There is no theology for the believer in Jesus Christ without the cross. Without God's example and sacrifice at the cross,nothing makes any sense for us. One of the most important lessons we learn from the cross is that love moves in two directions: vertical toward God and horizontal toward people. Jesus stretched out His arms to prove both at once. True spirituality connects worship and relationship. You can't reach up to God while pushing people away.

PASTOR PUTS IT LIKE THIS

If your worship goes up, but your love doesn't reach out, your love is lopsided. In this stead, the cross isn't just a symbol, it's a shape for what the Christian faith looks like. As a believer in Jesus Christ, hold fast to this one emphatic principle: keep your vertical tight and your horizontal right. When both line up, you form a cross-shaped love that changes lives.

THINK ABOUT IT FOR A MOMENT

- Is my love balanced between God and people?
- "Cross-shaped love connects Heaven and humanity."
- You can't claim the cross and ignore the crowd.

PRAY ABOUT IT

Lord, help me keep my love balanced. Let my worship for You spill over into compassion for others.

In the name of Jesus, Amen!

DAY 6: "The Hardest Love to Give"

STRAIGHT FROM THE BOOK

If a man say, I love God, and hateth his brother, he is a liar: for he that loveth not his brother whom he hath seen, how can he love God whom he hath not seen?

(1 John 4:20, KJV)

JESUS SAID IT BEST

Jesus told us to love our enemies and pray for those who persecute us. That's not easy love, that's supernatural love. Loving difficult people proves divine power. In short, it's love that requires the presence, power and potency of the Holy Spirit. He empowers us to love by fueling us with who He is to make it happen. The same God who loved you at your worst asks you to love others with the same kind of love that He loved you with.

PASTOR PUTS IT LIKE THIS

Let's be real for a moment. Some people are hard to love! But that's where the Holy Ghost shows off. Please keep this in mind, loving the unlovable does not make you weak; it makes you look like Jesus! When you forgive the ones who hurt you, Heaven shouts, "you look like Him" and hell shakes and says, "not another who acts like Jesus, we've got to stop them!"

THINK ABOUT IT FOR A MOMENT

- Who's the hardest person for me to love right now?
- "You can't spell G.R.A.C.E. without F.O.R.G.I.V.E."
- Hard love grows holy hearts.

PRAY ABOUT IT

Lord, help me love beyond my limits. Fill me with the strength to show grace where my flesh wants revenge.

In the name of Jesus, Amen!

Section III – Week Four

DAY 7: "Love Is My Testimony"

STRAIGHT FROM THE BOOK

If a man say, I love God, and hateth his brother, he is a liar: for he that loveth not his brother whom he hath seen, how can he love God whom he hath not seen?

(1 John 4:20, KJV)

JESUS SAID IT BEST

A testimony is best defined as the story that is attached to a test that was permitted by the Lord that caused growth, development and trust in a believer's heart for God. With this in mind, there are various kinds of tests, so there are different types of testimonies. However, your loudest testimony should always be love! Your love should be loud, bold and on public display for others to encounter. People may not remember your sermon, but they'll never forget your smile. Jesus said love would be the evidence of discipleship. Every act of love is a living testimony that God still transforms hearts.

PASTOR PUTS IT LIKE THIS

As a believer in Jesus Christ, you do not have to run around telling everybody that you love Jesus. Just learn to love like it! You don't have to tell everybody you're saved. Just act like it! Please hear this and let this live in your soul forever, let your love do the talking. Every time you help, hug, forgive, or feed somebody, that's a testimony walking on two legs. Some folks won't step foot in a church, but they'll read your life. Make it a love story.

THINK ABOUT IT FOR A MOMENT
- What does my love say about my faith?
- "Love preaches louder than a microphone ever could."
- Your life might be the only Bible some people ever read.

PRAY ABOUT IT

Lord, let my love testify. Let how I live make it easy for others to believe in You.

In the name of Jesus, Amen!

CONCLUSION | WEEK FOUR | 1 JOHN 4:20

As We Conclude Week *Four*...

This week we examined the challenging yet transformative truth found in 1 John 4:20, where the Apostle John confronts the disconnect between claiming to love God and refusing to love others. Believers in the faith should now understand that authentic love for God cannot exist without active love for people. The verse teaches us that love for God and love for neighbors are inseparably tied together. In fact, one validates the other.

This week revealed that our relationships with others are spiritual mirrors that reflect the condition of our relationship with God. It is easy to profess love for an invisible God, but the real test is seen in how we treat the people who stand in front of us. If love is absent horizontally, it cannot be genuine vertically. God calls His children to live out their faith by loving others with sincerity, maturity, and grace.

WHAT WE LEARNED THIS WEEK

1. Love for God Cannot Be Separated From Love for Others (1 John 4:20)

We learned that God rejects any claim to love Him that is not backed by love for others. True spirituality is demonstrated through relationships.

2. Hatred Toward People Contradicts the Claim of Loving God (1 John 4:20)

This week taught us that harboring bitterness, unforgiveness, or hatred reveals a heart that has not fully embraced God's love.

3. Our Love for God is Proven Through Our Love for People (1 John 4:20)

We discovered that loving others is not optional. It is evidence of divine transformation. When we love people, we reveal the work of God in our hearts.

4. God's Love Empowers Us to Love Difficult People (1 John 4:11)

We learned that loving others, even those who hurt us or frustrate us, is possible only because God loves us first and fills us with His love.

5. Love is the True Test of Christian Maturity (John 13:35)

This week revealed that spiritual maturity is not measured by gifts, knowledge, titles, or church involvement. It is measured by how well we love.

WEEK *Four* TAKEAWAYS

- My love for others reveals the authenticity of my love for God.
- If I claim to love God, I must also love the people He created.
- Hatred and love cannot coexist in a heart shaped by Christ.
- God empowers me to love even when loving is difficult.
- Love is evidence of spiritual maturity and true discipleship.
- How I treat others reflects the condition of my walk with God.

- Loving others is a command, not a suggestion and God gives grace to obey.

WEEK *Four* FINAL PRAYER

Father, thank You for teaching us the truth that loving You is inseparably connected to loving others. As we conclude Week Four of Section III, help us to walk in a love that honors You. Remove bitterness, heal wounds, and soften our hearts toward those we struggle to love. Fill us with Your Spirit so that our words, actions, and attitudes reflect the love of Christ. Teach us to love sincerely, to forgive freely, and to treat others with grace. May our relationships prove that Your love is real within us. In Jesus' name, Amen.

SECTION IV - *Week One*

DAY 1: THE GROUP ENCOUNTER

THERE'S NOTHING LIKE HIS LOVE FOR ME!

Scripture Lesson: Romans 5:8

Today's Subject: IT'S ALL ABOUT HIM!

KEY POINTS FROM TODAY'S LESSON

Point 1

_____

_____

_____

_____

_____

Point 2

_____

_____

_____

_____

_____

Point 3

_____

_____

_____

_____

_____

Here's What I'm Praying For Right Now:

_____

_____

_____

_____

_____

_____

_____

_____

DAY 2: "Love While I Was Wrong"

STRAIGHT FROM THE BOOK

But God commendeth his love toward us, in that, while we were yet sinners, Christ died for us. (Romans 5:8, KJV)

JESUS SAID IT BEST

The root of redemption rests in the fact that our salvation is God's work for us and not our work for Him. In other words, God didn't wait for us to get right with Him before He reached for us. The passage above suggests the following, "….while we were yet sinners…" The report from our Lord is that God loved us when we were not lovable at all! He loved us at our worst. Jesus died for people who denied Him, doubted Him, and disobeyed Him. That's divine love at its best.

PASTOR PUTS IT LIKE THIS

One of the most overwhelming things about God's love for us is that, it is not predicated on our love for Him in return. God's love for us is based on His sovereign decision to love us. Here's the shout, God made up His mind to love us and nothing is going to change His mind. You know it's real love when somebody loves you while you're still wrong. That's what God did! He loved you through your rebellion, through your bad decisions, through your "don't care" days. Love didn't wait for your turnaround, love caused it.

THINK ABOUT IT FOR A MOMENT

- Who else would love me like that?
- "Grace saw the mess and called it a masterpiece."
- God didn't fall in love with your perfection; He fell in love with your potential.

PRAY ABOUT IT

Lord, thank You for loving me before I ever got it together. Your love met me in my mess and brought me out.

In the name of Jesus, Amen!

DAY 3: "The Cost of Love"

STRAIGHT FROM THE BOOK

But God commendeth his love toward us, in that, while we were yet sinners, Christ died for us. (Romans 5:8, KJV)

JESUS SAID IT BEST

Real leather is expensive. Real diamonds cost an arm and a leg. Real pearls will make you want to find an oyster at the bottom of the sea and harvest it yourself. Real love is never ever cheap. It's always expensive. Jesus' love cost Him the praises of angels for the curses of sinful men. It cost Him the golden streets of glory for the dusty streets of Galilee. It costs Him His comfort, His crown, and His life. The cross was love's receipt and proof that God meant what He said. He didn't love in theory; He loved in blood.

PASTOR PUTS IT LIKE THIS

Please hold this principle close to your heart and retain it forever, love is not cheap! God paid full price for you! When Jesus could've walked away, He stayed on the cross. When He could've judged you, He justified you with His own blood. Every nail that was pierced in His body said, "you're worth it!" The cross was expensive, but He said, "charge it to My grace."

THINK ABOUT IT FOR A MOMENT

- How do I honor the cost God paid for me?
- "Love gives until it feels it, and then gives a little more."
- You were too valuable to be discounted.

PRAY ABOUT IT

Lord, thank You for paying the full price for my salvation. Let my life reflect the value You saw in me.

In the name of Jesus, Amen!

DAY 4: "Unstoppable Love"

STRAIGHT FROM THE BOOK

But God commendeth his love toward us, in that, while we were yet sinners, Christ died for us. (Romans 5:8, KJV)

JESUS SAID IT BEST

Nothing stopped God from loving you: not sin, not shame, and not separation. Not rebellion, regression, disobedience, lawlessness, missing the mark or even spiritual arrogance. Jesus faced betrayal, denial, and crucifixion, but love refused to quit. Romans 8 says, "Nothing shall separate us from the love of God." This suggests that His love was offered because He had a point that He had to prove. And that point was that His love at its core is absolutely unstoppable.

PASTOR PUTS IT LIKE THIS

When you sign a lease agreement, they make you sign a "No Quit Clause." It's a legal promise that says you will not quit until the lease is satisfied. When Jesus died at the cross that fateful Friday(,) He signed a "no quit" with his own blood. God's love got a no-quit clause! You can run, rebel, or resist, but love will still find you. You can't out-sin, out-run, or outlive it. It's unstoppable. Even when you ghosted God, His grace still texted, "I'm here."

THINK ABOUT IT FOR A MOMENT

- What tried to stop God's love from reaching me, but couldn't?
- "Love is undefeated! Over 2000 years later, we are still winning!"
- The grave couldn't hold it, and your guilt can't block it.

PRAY ABOUT IT

Lord, thank You that Your love never gives up on me. Teach me to love others with that same unstoppable spirit.

In The Name of Jesus, Amen!

DAY 5: "The Love That Changed Everything"

STRAIGHT FROM THE BOOK

But God commendeth his love toward us, in that, while we were yet sinners, Christ died for us. (Romans 5:8, KJV)

JESUS SAID IT BEST

The term "commendeth" used in the passage has a very rich meaning. It comes from the Greek word *synistemi*. It means to stand in concert with someone. It was used by Roman soldiers on the field of battle when they would stand with each other until victory was won. The moment Jesus said, "It is finished," it was His way of saying, "I stand with you and for you with my love that will change human history forever." The love of His cross turned sinners into sons, guilt into grace, and judgment into joy. God's love didn't just save you, it stood with you for the purpose of redeeming you from your sins.

PASTOR PUTS IT LIKE THIS

Here's the shout of the day, the love of Jesus Christ expressed at the cross was not just love unto His death, but it was a divine takeover! Love walked into the courtroom of eternal justice, stepped into the place of judgement, took your sentence, and then deleted your entire case file. You don't owe the devil an apology. You owe God a praise! Everything changed when His love showed up.

THINK ABOUT IT FOR A MOMENT

- What part of my life changed because of God's love?
- "Grace doesn't just forgive you; it refashions you."
- You're living proof that love works.

PRAY ABOUT IT

Lord, thank You for the love that changed everything about me. I'll live like someone who's been redeemed by grace.

In the name of Jesus, Amen!

DAY 6: "Love at First Cross"

STRAIGHT FROM THE BOOK

But God commendeth his love toward us, in that, while we were yet sinners, Christ died for us. (Romans 5:8, KJV)

JESUS SAID IT BEST

The quote, "Love at first sight" finds its root in the ancient wisdom writings of Egypt. In short, the quote is really old. It has made its way through the annals of time and has influenced the way we see and feel about things that are mentioned first. With this in mind, when it comes to love, God has a monopoly on the subject matter. He, alone, is the source of it. If you ever doubt God's love, look back at the cross. That's the moment Heaven said, "I love you," and hell couldn't argue with it. The cross was love's first public declaration and its final word.

PASTOR PUTS IT LIKE THIS

Not long ago, I heard a sermon declared by a friend of mine who said, "forget love at first sight, the Gospel gives us love at first cross!" You were on His mind before you were on this planet. With this in mind, the cross wasn't an accident; it was an announcement. It was God's Word to the world that said, "I'm committed to you forever and I love you!"

THINK ABOUT IT FOR A MOMENT

- How does the cross define love for me today?
- "The cross is proof that love is louder than sin."
- Every scar in His hand has your name written in it.

PRAY ABOUT IT

Lord, remind me that the cross was never just a story. It was always my story. Thank You for loving me first, best, and forever.

In the name of Jesus, Amen!

DAY 7: "Love That Won't Stay Dead"

STRAIGHT FROM THE BOOK

But God commendeth his love toward us, in that, while we were yet sinners, Christ died for us. (Romans 5:8, KJV)

JESUS SAID IT BEST

Love didn't stop at the cross, it kept going through the grave. The resurrection is proof that love always wins! Jesus didn't just die for you; He got up for you! Death lost, sin lost, shame lost and yet love still reigns.

PASTOR PUTS IT LIKE THIS

As a believer in Jesus Christ, there are some things that you should always remember about the cross of our Lord. In this vein, I contend that what took place that fateful weekend can be summed up like this: Friday showed us His pain, Saturday showed us His pause, but Sunday morning showed us His power! The same love that went down in defeat rose in total victory for those of us who believe. You can't keep love buried. It'll always rise again. That's why real love won't stay dead. It keeps getting up after you, kill it!

THINK ABOUT IT FOR A MOMENT

- What in my life needs resurrection love today?
- "Love rolled the stone away."
- If Jesus got up, so can you.

PRAY ABOUT IT

Lord, thank You that love rose with power. Because You live, I live and I'll spend my life loving You back.

In the name of Jesus, Amen!

CONCLUSION | WEEK ONE | ROMANS 5:8

As We Conclude Week *One*...

This week, we embraced the life-changing truth found in Romans 5:8, where the Apostle Paul unfolds the depth of God's love demonstrated toward humanity. Believers should now understand that God did not wait for us to get better, become worthy, or rise to righteousness before extending His love. Instead, He proved His love at the very moment we were at our worst, "while we were yet sinners." This week reminded us that divine love is proactive, sacrificial, and undeserved.

We learned that God's love is not merely spoken; it is shown. The cross stands as the eternal evidence that God values us, pursues us, and refuses to abandon us, even when we fail Him. His love does not fluctuate based on our behavior, nor does it diminish or decrease because of our shortcomings. God loved us fully, freely, and faithfully long before we ever thought about loving Him in return. Please retain this one radical truth: God loved us first!

This study revealed that understanding God's love transforms how we see ourselves, how we value our lives, and how we extend grace to others. When we grasp the magnitude of His love, shame loses its power, condemnation loses its voice, and insecurity loses its grip. God's love becomes the foundation on which we stand, the mirror that shapes our identity, and the motivation behind how we live, serve, and love.

WHAT WE LEARNED THIS WEEK

1. God Proved His Love While We Were Still Sinners (Romans 5:8)

We learned that God's love is demonstrated, not merely declared. The cross shows that God made the first move toward us when we had nothing to offer.

2. God's Love is Not Based on Our Performance (Romans 5:8)

This week taught us that we are loved at our lowest, not just at our best. His love is constant, unwavering, and not dependent on our perfection.

3. Christ's Sacrifice Reveals the Value God Places on Us (Romans 5:8)

We discovered that the price paid by Christ, Himself, shows how precious we are to God. Our worth is determined by His love, not our mistakes.

4. God's Love Removes Condemnation and Shame (Romans 8:1)

We learned that because of Christ, we no longer live under guilt or fear. His love lifts us, restores us, and gives us the freedom to walk in grace.

5. God's Love Calls Us to Extend Grace to Others (Ephesians 4:32)

This week revealed that as recipients of divine mercy, we must reflect that mercy in how we treat others. With this in mind, we should offer others forgiveness, patience, and compassion.

WEEK *One* TAKEAWAYS

- God loved me long before I ever loved Him.
- The cross is the permanent proof of God's love for me.
- My failures do not cancel God's affection toward me.
- Christ died for me at my worst, not my best.
- God's love establishes my worth and identity.
- Because God gave me grace, I must give grace to others.
- I can live free from guilt, shame, and fear because I am loved.

WEEK *One* FINAL PRAYER

Father, thank You for the transforming truth revealed in Romans 5:8. As we conclude Week Four of Section IV, remind us daily that Your love is not earned but freely given. Thank You for proving Your love through Christ's sacrifice on the cross. Help us to rest in that love, walk in that love, and reflect that love in every relationship we encounter. Heal every wound shaped by guilt, shame, or rejection. Teach us to see ourselves as You see us, deeply valued and fully loved. May the power of Your love strengthen us, guide us, and shape how we live. In Jesus' name, Amen.

SECTION IV - *Week Two*

DAY 1: THE GROUP ENCOUNTER

THERE'S NOTHING LIKE HIS LOVE FOR ME!

Scripture Lesson: St. John 3:16

Today's Subject: HE WANTED ME TO HAVE IT!

KEY POINTS FROM TODAY'S LESSON

Point 1

_____

_____

_____

_____

_____

Point 2

_____

_____

_____

_____

_____

Point 3

_____

_____

_____

_____

_____

_____

Here's What I'm Praying For Right Now:

_____

_____

_____

_____

_____

_____

_____

_____

DAY 2: "It Keeps On Giving"

STRAIGHT FROM THE BOOK

For God so loved the world, that he gave his only begotten Son, that whosoever believeth in him should not perish, but have everlasting life. (John 3:16, KJV)

JESUS SAID IT BEST

The ways of Jesus Christ have made it clear through the scriptures that "love" and "give" are synonyms. In short, love that's real will always give. In other words, God didn't just feel love; He followed through with it. The gift of His Son was the proof of His heart. Jesus wasn't forced, He was offered. There's a big difference between these two idiomatic ideas. Love that gives is love that costs something.

PASTOR PUTS IT LIKE THIS

There are times we hear people say, "I love you" and it's just talk. Not long ago, I told one of the members of the Antioch Church, "I love you my friend." To my surprise that member looked at me with the biggest smile I've ever seen and said, "Prove it!" Keep this in mind, love doesn't just talk, it transfers. God didn't send a text message from Heaven; He sent His Son! That's the ultimate giveaway. Love always gives its best, not its leftovers. And if God gave Jesus for you, what makes you think He won't take care of the rest?

THINK ABOUT IT FOR A MOMENT

- How do I show love through giving?
- "You can give without loving, but you can't love without giving."
- The size of your gift reveals the size of your heart.

PRAY ABOUT IT

Lord, thank You for giving Jesus. Teach me to give like You: freely, faithfully, and full of love.

In the name of Jesus, Amen!

DAY 3: "Accept the Invitation"

STRAIGHT FROM THE BOOK

For God so loved the world, that he gave his only begotten Son, that whosoever believeth in him should not perish, but have everlasting life. (John 3:16, KJV)

JESUS SAID IT BEST

The Gospel is an open invitation. Hear the word of this passage that embraces every fallen person on the planet. Jesus said, "...that whosoever believeth..." This means anybody, anywhere, anytime. God's love doesn't discriminate like we do. Jesus made sure the door stayed open for the broken, the outcast, and the forgotten. He made room for the least, last, leftover, left out and the left behind. The only requirement is belief.

PASTOR PUTS IT LIKE THIS

Here's the shout of the day, the "whosoever" of Jesus Christ includes you! Not the flawless, perfect, renewed and redeemed you, but the fallen you. That means no matter what your past, your pain, or your personal profile, you're in the plan! Your flaws have been factored in! Keep this in mind, religion draws circles to keep people out; Jesus draws bigger ones to pull people in. Here's the best news ever, if you're still breathing, you're still invited!

THINK ABOUT IT FOR A MOMENT

- Do I believe God's love truly includes me?
- "You're the 'whosoever' He was talking about."
- The door to grace never closes.

PRAY ABOUT IT

Lord, thank You that Your love is for everybody, including a person like me. Let me live like someone fully accepted by grace.

In the name of Jesus, Amen!

DAY 4: "It Really Saves"

STRAIGHT FROM THE BOOK

For God so loved the world, that he gave his only begotten Son, that whosoever believeth in him should not perish, but have everlasting life. (John 3:16, KJV)

JESUS SAID IT BEST

Jesus showed us what His love was like because He perpetually reached out to save people. With this in mind, God's love didn't just reach you, it rescued you! His love doesn't just comfort; it saves. The word perish means "to be destroyed," It suggests that something has been burned into ashes; however, the cross canceled that outcome! Eternal life isn't just about Heaven later, it's about new life now.

PASTOR PUTS IT LIKE THIS

If you ever wonder how much you're worth, check the receipt! The cross says, "Paid in Full." Love snatched you from what you deserved and delivered you to what you didn't. Salvation isn't God's backup plan; it's His love plan. I have made this statement over and over again, and for the purpose of redundancy and clarity, I will say it again, your salvation is not about what you have done for God, it is about what God has done for you that you could have done without Him!

THINK ABOUT IT FOR A MOMENT

- What has God's love saved me from?
- "You can't out-sin salvation's reach."
- The cross erased your expiration date.

PRAY ABOUT IT

Lord, thank You that Your love didn't just find me, it saved me. Help me live grateful for a salvation I could never earn.

In the name of Jesus, Amen!

DAY 5: "He Made a Believer Out of Me"

STRAIGHT FROM THE BOOK

For God so loved the world, that he gave his only begotten Son, that whosoever believeth in him should not perish, but have everlasting life. (John 3:16, KJV)

JESUS SAID IT BEST

God's love doesn't end at the grave. Jesus said, "I am the resurrection and the life." His love is eternal in that it outlasts time, trials, and tears. Every believer carries the promise of forever love: unbroken fellowship with God through Christ. With this in mind, what Jesus Christ really does is makes believers out of us by loving us perpetually and continually.

PASTOR PUTS IT LIKE THIS

The love of God is not like a flight that can't take off in bad weather so they cancel it. His love is not like a check written on a checking account that has been canceled due to insufficient funds. His love is always good! Here's the shout of the day. You can't cancel eternal love! God's love doesn't expire, evaporate, or fade out like a cell phone in a bad spot. You may change, but His love stays logged in. The same love that got you through this week will guide you through eternity!

THINK ABOUT IT FOR A MOMENT

- How does it feel knowing God's love lasts forever?
- "Eternal life is just love that never clocks out."
- Heaven is the home address of God's love.

PRAY ABOUT IT

Lord, thank You for love that outlasts everything else. Help me live today in light of forever with You.

In the name of Jesus, Amen!

DAY 6: "The One and Only"

STRAIGHT FROM THE BOOK

For God so loved the world, that he gave his only begotten Son, that whosoever believeth in him should not perish, but have everlasting life. (John 3:16, KJV)

JESUS SAID IT BEST

All too often, we treat Jesus like He is an item on a buffet line that can be compared to other things, people and places. However, when you study the scriptures, the Bible makes it very clear that Jesus wasn't one of many, He was the one and only. God gave Heaven's best so you could have life at its best. His "only Son" shows us just how precious you are to Him! God didn't send an angel; He peeled off divinity and wrapped Himself in humanity just to show us just how much He truly loved us.

PASTOR PUTS IT LIKE THIS

I often hate eating at restaurants just before closing time. It's because they are guilty of often serving you what I call "sloppy seconds." When you consider the death of Jesus Christ at the cross, you have to conclude that He was Heaven's absolute best! He was not a "sloppy second". He was the one and only! That's how much you matter to God! He didn't reach into Heaven's leftovers; He gave His first and finest. If you ever question your worth, look at what He was willing to trade for you! Jesus is the proof that you're priceless.

THINK ABOUT IT FOR A MOMENT

- What does the phrase "only Son" tell me about God's love?
- "Your value is measured by what was paid for you."
- Heaven went bankrupt to redeem you.

PRAY ABOUT IT

Lord, thank You for sending Your only Son for me. Help me never treat lightly what cost You everything.

In the name of Jesus, Amen!

DAY 7: "Lottie, Dottie, and Everybody"

STRAIGHT FROM THE BOOK

For God so loved the world, that he gave his only begotten Son, that whosoever believeth in him should not perish, but have everlasting life. (John 3:16, KJV)

JESUS SAID IT BEST

The reach of God's love is transglobal. He didn't just love Israel, He loved the world. That means His love includes every tribe, tongue, and time zone. The same love that reached the thief on the cross can reach the single mom, the addict, the skeptic, and the saint.

PASTOR PUTS IT LIKE THIS

God's love is too big for borders. He's got love for everybody, from the pulpit to the prison yard, from the suburbs to the streets of the inner-city. You can't place into a religious sect and strap Him to a pew. God's love is too much for you to contain, retain or explain. God's love for us is the one thing that will never stay local.

THINK ABOUT IT FOR A MOMENT

- How wide is God's love in my view of others?
- "The world is loved, no exceptions."
- If God's love is global, so should mine be.

PRAY ABOUT IT

Lord, thank You that Your love wraps around the whole world which includes me. Help me spread it wherever I go.

In the name of Jesus, Amen!

CONCLUSION | WEEK TWO | JOHN 3:16
As We Conclude Week *Two*…

This week, we reflected on one of the most beloved and foundational verses in all of Scripture, St. John 3:16. In this single sentence, Jesus reveals the breadth, depth, and intention of God's love toward humanity. Students of the faith should now understand that the love of God is not abstract, partial, or passive. It is intentional, sacrificial, and universal. God loved the world so completely that He gave His only begotten Son, by offering salvation to anyone who believes.

We learned that the heart of the gospel is not condemnation, but compassion. God's motive was love, His method was giving, and His mission was saving. This week reminded us that divine love does not merely observe the human condition, it intervenes to redeem it. God's love is global in scope yet personal in application. It reaches the world but embraces each of us individually.

This study showed us that eternal life is not earned; it is received by believing in the One whom God sent. Through Christ, we discover the true nature of God's heart, a love that withholds nothing, sacrifices everything, and invites everyone. John 3:16 is not just a verse to memorize; it is a truth to live by, rest in, share, and celebrate.

WHAT WE LEARNED THIS WEEK

1. God's Love Motivated His Gift of Salvation (John 3:16)

We learned that God's primary motive toward humanity is love. Everything He does flows from the richness of His heart toward us.

2. God Gave His Only Begotten Son as the Ultimate Demonstration of Love (John 3:16)

This week taught us that divine love is proven through giving. God held nothing back, not even His only Son.

3. Salvation is Offered to "Whosoever" Believes (John 3:16)

We discovered that God's offer of eternal life is inclusive and available to all. No background, mistake, or past failure disqualifies anyone from receiving His grace.

4. Eternal Life Comes Through Faith in Christ Alone (John 3:16; John 14:6)

We learned that eternal life is not a reward for good works; it is a gift received through believing in Jesus as Savior and Lord.

5. God's Mission is to Save, Not Condemn (John 3:17)

This week revealed that God's desire is restoration, not rejection. He extends love before judgment, mercy before accountability, and grace before discipline.

WEEK *Two* TAKEAWAYS

- God's love for the world includes me, personally.
- Divine love is proven through God giving His Son.
- Salvation is available to anyone who believes.
- Eternal life is a gift, not an achievement.
- God's heart is to save, not to condemn.
- My faith in Christ gives me access to everlasting life.
- I am called to share God's love with confidence and compassion.

WEEK *Two* FINAL PRAYER

Father, thank You for the life-changing truth of John 3:16. As we conclude Week Two of Section IV, let the reality of Your love settle deeply into our hearts. Thank You for giving Your only begotten Son so that we might have eternal life. Teach us to embrace this gift with gratitude, to live in it with confidence, and to share it with others boldly. Help us to remember that Your love is for the world, yet also for each of us, personally. May this truth strengthen our faith, deepen our devotion, and inspire our service. In Jesus' name, Amen.

SECTION IV - *Week Three*

DAY 1: THE GROUP ENCOUNTER

THERE'S NOTHING LIKE HIS LOVE FOR ME!

Scripture Lesson: Isaiah 53:5-8

Today's Subject: WE HAD A SUBSTITUTE TODAY!

KEY POINTS FROM TODAY'S LESSON

Point 1

_____

_____

_____

_____

_____

_____

Point 2

_____

_____

_____

_____

_____

Point 3

_____

_____

_____

_____

_____

_____

Here's What I'm Praying For Right Now:

_____

_____

_____

_____

_____

_____

_____

_____

DAY 2: "Welcome to the Courtroom"

STRAIGHT FROM THE BOOK

He was taken from prison and from judgment: And who shall declare his generation? For he was cut off out of the land of the living: For the transgression of my people was he stricken. (Isaiah 53:8, KJV)

JESUS SAID IT BEST

When the scriptures record, "He was taken from prison…", the scene is that of a lamb entering into a courtroom. These words, though spoken through Isaiah, offered us a picture perfect prophecy of what was yet to come in the person of Jesus Christ. The Lamb of God stood in the courtroom of injustice: silent, surrendered, and still loving. He accepted prison so you could experience freedom. Love doesn't look for loopholes; it stands in your place.

PASTOR PUTS IT LIKE THIS

The story was told of a man walking into the prison with handcuffs and standing before a just judge. There was also a man on death row awaiting execution. The man on death row was exonerated and released to go free! When the guilty man got outside, he was met by the judge who told him that he was able to go free because the man he saw enter wearing handcuffs took his place. The judge told the man, on death row, that the man who took His place was His son! Here's the shout, they locked Him up so you could live free! Love went to court. Love took the punishment. Love served the sentence.

THINK ABOUT IT FOR A MOMENT

- Where was I imprisoned before love set me free?
- "He took my cuffs so I could lift my hands."

PRAY ABOUT IT

Lord, thank You for breaking my chains. Help me never go back to what You've already freed me from.

In The Name of Jesus, Amen!

DAY 3: "I've Been Reconnected"

STRAIGHT FROM THE BOOK

He was taken from prison and from judgment: And who shall declare his generation? For he was cut off out of the land of the living: For the transgression of my people was he stricken. (Isaiah 53:8, KJV)

JESUS SAID IT BEST

When Jesus died on the cross, He cried out, "My God, my God why hath thou forsaken me?" (St. Matt. 27:46). It was at that moment He became sin for us and was separated from His Father in Heaven for the first time ever. With this in mind, Jesus was "cut off" so you could be brought in. He experienced separation from the Father so you could enjoy eternal connection. When He cried, "my God, why hast Thou forsaken Me?" that was love bridging the gap between holiness and humanity.

PASTOR PUTS IT LIKE THIS

We live in a culture filled with things that are often disconnected. Phone calls drop, lights can get turned off and water bills, if not paid, can cause city workers to disconnect it. But Jesus took the disconnect so you could stay connected! Love took the hit and built the hotline. You've got lifetime coverage and unlimited minutes with Heaven. When He got cut off on the cross, the veil in the temple ripped wide open. Now access is free and forever.

THINK ABOUT IT FOR A MOMENT

- How has Jesus' sacrifice connected me to God?
- "Love tore the curtain so grace could walk in."
- You're never out of range of God's signal.

PRAY ABOUT IT

Lord, thank You for reconnecting me when sin had cut me off. Keep me close to You every day.

In the name of Jesus, Amen!

DAY 4: "Silence of the Lamb"

STRAIGHT FROM THE BOOK

He was taken from prison and from judgment: And who shall declare his generation? For he was cut off out of the land of the living: For the transgression of my people was he stricken. (Isaiah 53:8, KJV)

JESUS SAID IT BEST

When accused, Jesus opened not His mouth. Silence became the sound of submission. Love doesn't always have to defend itself, sometimes it just endures! The silence expressed by the Lamb, in our study passage, displayed a divinely inspired quiet (Isaiah 53:5-8) that was not weakness; it was willingness.

PASTOR PUTS IT LIKE THIS

I love movies. In fact, I consider myself to be a movie buff. One of my favorite films of all time is the thriller *Silence of the Lambs.* Each time, I have watched it my mind has raced to this passage because Jesus was the first silent lamb that time has ever seen. Here's the shout, Jesus had plenty to say. But on that day He held His peace. What He wanted to say was what He was currently doing: loving the unlovable! He could've called angels, but He chose silence. Love sometimes proves itself by what it doesn't say. When you know the outcome belongs to God, you can hush and let Heaven handle it.

THINK ABOUT IT FOR A MOMENT

- Where do I need to let love speak through silence?
- "Silence under pressure is strength under control."
- Love doesn't always shout. Sometimes it bleeds quietly.

PRAY ABOUT IT

Lord, give me the strength to stay silent when grace is louder than words.

In the name of Jesus, Amen!

DAY 5: "Stricken but Still Strong"

STRAIGHT FROM THE BOOK

He was taken from prison and from judgment: And who shall declare his generation? For he was cut off out of the land of the living: For the transgression of my people was he stricken. (Isaiah 53:8, KJV)

JESUS SAID IT BEST

To be beaten is one thing, but to be broken is another. Isaiah reveals that love took a beating but never broke. Jesus took humanity's worst so He could offer heaven's best. Even stricken, He stayed strong because love always finishes what it starts.

PASTOR PUTS IT LIKE THIS

This prophetic picture of the suffering of our Savior Jesus Christ is one of the most gruesome and horrible that time has ever recorded. They hit Him, hurt Him, and hung Him on a tree while He was still alive and that could not stop Him! That's what real love does. It takes the blows and keeps blessing. Next time life hits you hard, remember: you've got resurrection DNA in your spirit. Love might look wounded, but it is still going to win in the end!

THINK ABOUT IT FOR A MOMENT

- How has God's strength shown up in my own suffering?
- "If love survived Calvary, it'll survive my chaos."
- Stricken doesn't mean stopped.

PRAY ABOUT IT

Lord, thank You that love stays strong even when life gets hard. Help me to endure like You did.

In the name of Jesus, Amen!

DAY 6: "He Took My Place"

STRAIGHT FROM THE BOOK

He was taken from prison and from judgment: And who shall declare his generation? For he was cut off out of the land of the living: For the transgression of my people was he stricken. (Isaiah 53:8, KJV)

JESUS SAID IT BEST

Our study passage for the week has presented to us the raison d'etre of our faith as it pertains to the doctrine of substitution. This is the fundamental teaching throughout Christianity that Jesus Christ took our place at the cross. Jesus took your place so you could take His! He gave us His righteousness for our sin, His life for our death, His light for our darkness! That's not just love, it is a divine exchange.

PASTOR PUTS IT LIKE THIS

Once while teaching on the doctrine of substitution, a member raised a hand and said, "Pastor Adolph, you mean to tell me I was living on death row and I did not even know it?" I looked at this member and said not only were you on death row, but headed to hell wearing garments soaked in gasoline! Okay, I'm being a little dramatic, but I think you get the picture. Here's the best news of the day, love stepped in and said, "Switch seats with me." This is why the cross should be personal to you. Your name was written on His stripes. Every drop of blood screamed, "This one's Mine!"

THINK ABOUT IT FOR A MOMENT
- What does it mean that Jesus stood in my place?
- "He took my spot so I could take His standing."
- The exchange rate of grace is always in your favor.

PRAY ABOUT IT

Lord, thank You for standing in my place. Let me live every day like someone rescued by love.

In the name of Jesus, Amen!

DAY 7: "Let Me Tell You All About Him"

STRAIGHT FROM THE BOOK

He was taken from prison and from judgment: And who shall declare his generation? For he was cut off out of the land of the living: For the transgression of my people was he stricken. (Isaiah 53:8, KJV)

JESUS SAID IT BEST

Isaiah asked, "who will tell His story?" The resurrection answered that question, "we will". Love didn't die with Jesus; it lives in everyone who carries His message. The cross was not the end. It was the echo that still calls the world home. The words of Isaiah 53:5-8 are life changing when you consider that they are prophetic and paint a picture of our suffering Savior that was still yet to come. With this in mind, it gives every believer something to brag about when it concerns the person of Jesus Christ!

PASTOR PUTS IT LIKE THIS

There is an old hymn that used to be shared in worship services when I grew up in church as a young boy. The old saints would say, "I said I wasn't gonna tell nobody, but I couldn't keep it to myself!" That's what this verse is all about. Take a moment as this week of study ends and read Isaiah 53:5-8 and consider that after all that the Lord has done for you, it gives you a lot that you can share about Him regarding His love! With this in mind, every time you forgive, serve, preach, sing, or give, love keeps talking through you. Don't let the story go silent. Be the proof that Calvary still works.

THINK ABOUT IT FOR A MOMENT

- How can I "declare His generation" today?
- "Love never stopped speaking; it just switched mouths."
- The message still moves through you.

PRAY ABOUT IT

Lord, thank You for trusting me to carry the story of Your love. Let my life keep Your message alive.

In the name of Jesus, Amen!

CONCLUSION | WEEK THREE | ISAIAH 53:8

As We Conclude Week *Three*...

This week, we journeyed through the profound and prophetic words of Isaiah 53:8, a passage that unveils the suffering, sacrifice, and substitutionary work of the Messiah. Students of Scripture should now understand that this verse highlights the unjust treatment, silent submission, and redemptive purpose behind Christ's suffering. Isaiah reveals that Jesus was "taken from prison and from judgment," not because of His own wrongdoing, but because of ours. He endured oppression and affliction so that we might experience freedom and salvation.

We learned that the phrase "who shall declare His generation?" points to the tragedy of a life cut off prematurely, yet also to the triumph of a mission fulfilled perfectly. Christ bore the judgment that belonged to us and took upon Himself the penalty of sin so we could stand reconciled before God. His death was not an accident, nor was it a defeat, it was a divine exchange. The innocent suffered for the guilty, the righteous for the unrighteous, and the holy for the unholy.

This week reminded us that Christ's silence was not weakness but willingness. He did not resist the suffering brought against Him because He came to fulfill the Father's redemptive plan. In His suffering, we find healing. In His sacrifice, we find salvation. In His surrender, we find everlasting hope. Isaiah 53:8 teaches us that Jesus carried our story in His suffering, and through His death, He rewrote our destiny.

WHAT WE LEARNED THIS WEEK

1. Christ Was Taken from Judgment on Our Behalf (Isaiah 53:8)

We learned that Jesus endured unjust treatment because He willingly stepped into our place. What we deserved, He absorbed.

2. Jesus Suffered Silently as a Sign of His Surrender (Isaiah 53:7–8)

This week taught us that His silence was not powerlessness but purpose. He accepted suffering as part of His redeeming work.

3. Christ Was "Cut Off" for the Transgressions of God's People (Isaiah 53:8)

We discovered that His death was a substitutionary sacrifice. He died the death that belonged to us so we could receive the life that belongs to Him.

4. Redemption Required a Perfect Substitute (2 Corinthians 5:21)

We learned that salvation was made possible because the sinless One became sin for us, satisfying God's justice and expressing His love.

5. The Suffering of Christ Reveals Both God's Justice and His Mercy (Romans 3:23–26)

This week revealed that in the cross, wrath and grace meet. God judged sin but also extended mercy, proving His holiness and His compassion.

WEEK *Three* TAKEAWAYS

- Jesus took my place in judgment so I could take my place in grace.
- His suffering was purposeful, redemptive, and willingly embraced.
- Christ's silence in suffering reveals His commitment to save me.
- I am forgiven because He was "cut off" for my transgressions.
- Salvation required a perfect substitute and Jesus is that substitute.
- The cross shows both God's justice and His mercy working together.
- My new life is possible because Jesus gave His life for me.

WEEK *Three* FINAL PRAYER

Father, thank You for the powerful truth of Isaiah 53:8. As we conclude Week Three of Section IV, we pause in gratitude for the suffering Christ endured on our behalf. Thank You for a Savior who faced judgment silently, lovingly, and willingly so that we might be redeemed. Help us to live each day aware of the price paid for our salvation. Strengthen our faith through this truth, deepen our love because of His sacrifice, and increase our devotion to the One who gave everything for us. May our lives reflect the hope, freedom, and grace we have received through Jesus Christ. In His precious name, Amen.

SECTION IV - *Week Four*

DAY 1: THE GROUP ENCOUNTER

THERE'S NOTHING LIKE HIS LOVE FOR ME!

Scripture Lesson: St. John 15:13

Today's Subject: Everybody Ain't Your Friend!

KEY POINTS FROM TODAY'S LESSON

Point 1

_____

_____

_____

_____

_____

Point 2

_____

_____

_____

_____

_____

Point 3

_____

_____

_____

_____

_____

_____

_____

Here's What I'm Praying For Right Now:

_____

_____

_____

_____

_____

_____

_____

_____

DAY 2: "Greater Is Not Later, It's Now"

STRAIGHT FROM THE BOOK

Greater love hath no man than this, that a man lay down his life for his friends. (John 15:13, KJV)

JESUS SAID IT BEST

When Jesus declared, "greater love hath no man than this," He wasn't pointing His disciples toward a future moment they had to wait on. He was pointing them toward Himself. Jesus wanted them to understand that the greatest demonstration of love was already unfolding in their presence.

PASTOR PUTS IT LIKE THIS

Sometimes we sit around waiting for God to show us something bigger, deeper, or more powerful, not realizing He already revealed the greatest thing He could ever give, Himself. Greater isn't coming… greater came when Jesus stretched out His hands on the cross! That wasn't "starter love." That was the highest love Heaven had to offer. So stop expecting later what God has already provided now. You're walking in greater every day you wake up saved, redeemed, covered, and called. God didn't wait to love you. He loved you immediately, completely, and sacrificially. Greater is not on the way; greater is already yours.

THINK ABOUT IT FOR A MOMENT

- What if the "greater" you've been waiting on has already arrived?
- Jesus didn't delay love; He delivered it fully at Calvary.
- Sometimes the greatest blessing is recognizing what God has already done.

PRAY ABOUT IT

Lord, thank You for revealing the greatest expression of love right now through Jesus Christ. Help me to recognize and walk in the greatness of Your love today.

In the name of Jesus, Amen!

DAY 3: "It's Always Been a Love Thing"

STRAIGHT FROM THE BOOK

Greater love hath no man than this, that a man lay down his life for his friends. (John 15:13, KJV)

JESUS SAID IT BEST

Jesus made it clear in John 15:13 that everything God does flows from a single source, His love. Long before humanity ever responded to God, God had already set His love in motion. From creation to covenant, from the prophets to the cross, Jesus reveals that God's actions have always been motivated by love. Redemption wasn't a backup plan; it was love's plan. Forgiveness wasn't conditional; it was love's expression.

PASTOR PUTS IT LIKE THIS

If you ever want to understand God, start with love. Every blessing He gives, every door He opens, every sin He forgives, and every prayer He answers is rooted in love. God didn't start loving you when you got saved. He loved you before you ever knew His name. He loved you before your first breath, before your first mistake, before your first prayer. Everything He has ever done in your life, waking you up, protecting you, keeping you, redeeming you, has been a love thing.

THINK ABOUT IT FOR A MOMENT

- What would my life look like if I viewed everything God does as love in action?
- Love isn't something God switches on. It's who He is.
- From creation to salvation, the story has always been love.

PRAY ABOUT IT

Father, thank You for showing me that everything You have done in my life has always been rooted in love. Help me to see each blessing, each mercy, and each moment of grace as evidence of Your heart toward me.

In the name of Jesus, Amen!

DAY 4: "There's No Comparison"

STRAIGHT FROM THE BOOK

Greater love hath no man than this, that a man lay down his life for his friends. (John 15:13, KJV)

JESUS SAID IT BEST

Jesus' words, in John 15:13, draw a clear line between human love and divine love. Human love is beautiful, but it is flawed. With this in mind, sometimes it's inconsistent, sometimes it's conditional, and in many instances it is fragile. But Jesus offers a love that stands alone, unmatched and unrivaled. His willingness to lay down His life sets His love apart as incomparable. No one else can love with that level of purity, sacrifice, endurance, and commitment.

PASTOR PUTS IT LIKE THIS

Stop trying to compare God's love to the love of people. They're not even in the same category. People may change their minds, break their promises, withdraw their support, or fail you when life gets really rough. But here's the shout, Jesus never will! His love doesn't shift based on mood, moment, or mistake. His love stands strong through storms, weaknesses, and failures. When everyone else falls short, Jesus remains steady.

THINK ABOUT IT FOR A MOMENT

- Have I been comparing God's love to people's love?
- Human love fluctuates. Divine love is flawless.
- No earthly relationship can duplicate the love Jesus gives.

PRAY ABOUT IT

Lord, thank You for a love that cannot be compared or matched by anyone. Help me never to measure Your love by human standards, but to rest in the confidence that Your love is perfect, constant, and complete. Teach me to cherish Your love above all others.

In the name of Jesus, Amen!

DAY 5: "He Put His Life on the Line"

STRAIGHT FROM THE BOOK

Greater love hath no man than this, that a man lay down his life for his friends. (John 15:13, KJV)

JESUS SAID IT BEST

When Jesus spoke about laying down His life, He wasn't offering a metaphor. He was announcing His mission. He wanted His followers to know that His death wouldn't be accidental, but sacrificial. Jesus wasn't pushed to the cross; He willingly walked toward it. He put His life on the line because love demanded action, not theory. He saw humanity drowning in sin, and He stepped into danger to rescue us. His sacrifice wasn't forced, manipulated, or coerced. It was voluntary love.

PASTOR PUTS IT LIKE THIS

Jesus didn't just risk a little for you. He put everything on the line. He didn't love you from a distance. He stepped into your condition, carried your sins, and faced death head-on. That's what putting your life on the line looks like. He didn't die because He had to, He died because He wanted to redeem you. You were worth the blood! You were worth the sacrifice. You were worth the cross! That's why when life gets hard, you can stand tall and say, "Jesus proved His love for me." Nobody else has ever died to save your soul. Only Jesus put everything on the line to give you life.

THINK ABOUT IT FOR A MOMENT

- Jesus didn't risk something for me. He gave everything for me.
- The cross is the clearest picture of sacrificial love.
- If His love cost Him His life, my life should honor His love.

PRAY ABOUT IT

Jesus, thank You for laying down Your life for me. Help me to never take Your sacrifice lightly.

In the name of Jesus, Amen!

DAY 6: "There's Not a Friend"

STRAIGHT FROM THE BOOK

Greater love hath no man than this, that a man lay down his life for his friends. (John 15:13, KJV)

JESUS SAID IT BEST

Jesus shows us, in John 15:13, that true friendship isn't defined by words, convenience, or proximity. It's defined by sacrifice. There is no friend like Jesus because no one else has ever done what He has done for humanity. He understands us fully, loves us deeply, forgives us repeatedly, and stays with us constantly.

PASTOR PUTS IT LIKE THIS

You may have some good friends, but you don't have any friend like Jesus. He's the Friend who shows up when the room empties. He's the Friend who listens when no one else cares. He's the Friend who understands what you can't explain. He's the Friend who covers you when life exposes you. He's the Friend who never lies, never leaves, and never stops loving. Jesus is the Friend who comes through every time: in trouble, in tears, in weakness, in fear. And the greatest proof is this: He laid down His life just to call you friend. Nobody else loves like that!

THINK ABOUT IT FOR A MOMENT

- Who else knows me fully and loves me completely?
- No friend has ever done what Jesus has done.
- True friendship is proven through sacrifice — and Jesus proved it perfectly.

PRAY ABOUT IT

Lord Jesus, thank You for being the Friend who never fails, never abandons, and never stops loving me. Help me to lean into Your presence in every season of life. Teach me to trust You more deeply and to value Your friendship above all earthly connections.

In the name of Jesus, Amen!

DAY 7: "The Ship That Matters Most: Friendship"

STRAIGHT FROM THE BOOK

Greater love hath no man than this, that a man lay down his life for his friends. (John 15:13, KJV)

JESUS SAID IT BEST

In calling His disciples "friends," Jesus elevated their relationship beyond servanthood into intimacy. Friendship with Jesus is not shallow or superficial, it is anchored in revelation, sacrifice, and shared purpose. In John 15:13, He reveals that true friendship involves giving, sharing, and loving at the deepest level. Jesus didn't just call us friends; He proved it by laying down His life. He invites us into a relationship where He shares His heart, His truth, and His presence. Friendship with Jesus is the ship that carries believers through storms, trials, and transitions because it is grounded in unfailing love.

PASTOR PUTS IT LIKE THIS

Life has many "ships" in it. For example, there are relationships, partnerships, scholarships, fellowships, but the ship that will change your life forever is friendship with Jesus Christ! This is the ship that keeps you steady when everything else is shaking. This is the ship that guides you when life gets confusing. This is the ship that comforts you when the world gets cold. Jesus isn't just a Savior in your life; He is the Friend of your soul.

THINK ABOUT IT FOR A MOMENT

- Friendship with Jesus stabilizes every other "ship" in my life.
- When He calls me friend, He invites me into intimacy and purpose.
- This friendship is the anchor that holds me steady.

PRAY ABOUT IT

Lord, thank You for calling me Your friend and for offering a relationship built on love, grace, and truth. Help me to treasure this friendship and to walk closely with You each day. Let my life reflect the stability, joy, and peace that come from sailing with You.

In the name of Jesus, Amen!

<u>CONCLUSION | WEEK FOUR | JOHN 15:13</u>

As We Conclude Week *Four...*

This week we reflected upon the profound words of Jesus in John 15:13, a verse that reveals the highest expression of love ever demonstrated: the willingness to lay down one's life for another. Students of the faith should now understand that this passage is far more than a statement. It is a declaration of divine love, a foreshadowing of Calvary, and a call to embody sacrificial love in daily living. Jesus teaches that the greatest love is not merely spoken or shown in convenience but demonstrated through selfless sacrifice.

We learned that this verse points directly to Christ's atoning work on the cross, where He offered His life willingly and lovingly. His death was not forced, accidental, or circumstantial, it was intentional. The Good Shepherd laid down His life for the sheep. This week reminded us that divine love is both costly and courageous. Jesus did not love from afar. He entered our world, carried our burdens, bore our sins, and surrendered His life so that we might live.

This study revealed that as disciples, we are called to reflect this sacrificial love in our relationships. While we may not be asked to give our physical lives, we are required to lay down pride, selfishness, bitterness, and comfort for the sake of others. The love Jesus describes is active, not passive; voluntary, not reluctant; and transformative, not transactional. John 15:13 teaches us that real love imitates Christ. It costs something, gives something, and changes everything.

<u>WHAT WE LEARNED THIS WEEK</u>

1. The Greatest Love is Revealed Through Sacrifice (John 15:13)

We learned that love reaches its highest expression when someone willingly sacrifices for the good of another. Jesus defines greatness in love through giving, not receiving.

2. Jesus Laid Down His Life Willingly (John 10:17–18)

This week taught us that Christ's sacrifice was voluntary. No one took His life from Him. Jesus offered His life as the perfect demonstration of divine love.

3. Christ's Death was the Ultimate Act of Friendship (John 15:13–15)

We discovered that Jesus calls us friends, and His sacrificial death reveals the depth of His affection and commitment toward us.

4. Sacrificial Love is the Mark of True Discipleship (John 13:34–35)

We learned that Jesus expects His followers to love others the way He loves us selflessly, consistently, and sacrificially.

5. Love Requires Laying Something Down (Philippians 2:5–8)

This week revealed that sacrificial love may not always cost our lives, but it will cost our comfort, our pride, and our desire to be first. True love imitates Christ's humility and self-giving nature.

WEEK *Four* TAKEAWAYS

- The greatest expression of love is sacrifice.
- Jesus willingly gave His life to save mine.
- Christ's death demonstrates divine love and intimate friendship.
- Real discipleship is proven through sacrificial love.
- I am called to lay down pride, selfishness, and bitterness for others.
- Christ's love changes how I love the people around me.
- The cross is the ultimate example of how far love is willing to go.

WEEK *Four* FINAL PRAYER

Father, thank You for the powerful truth found in John 15:13. As we conclude Week Four of Section IV and complete this study, we stand in awe of the sacrificial love of Jesus Christ. Thank You for a Savior who laid down His life willingly, lovingly, and completely for us. Help us to embrace this love fully and reflect it faithfully. Teach us to love with courage, humility, and compassion. Strengthen us to lay aside anything that hinders us from loving others the way Christ has loved us. May the example of Jesus guide our hearts, shape our actions, and inspire our service. In His mighty and matchless name we pray, Amen.

CLOSING CHAPTER

LOVE STILL WINS

There are many stories we can tell about our walk with God. Stories of triumph and trial, gain and grief, strength and surrender. But, when all of those stories are gathered and written together, one truth stands out above them all. Love still wins!

From the very beginning, love has been God's greatest strategy and His strongest statement. It was love that spoke light into darkness, love that breathed life into dust, and love that refused to abandon a world that had walked away. When sin broke creation's heart, love volunteered for the rescue. And, when Jesus hung on the cross, love shouted louder than death.

This devotional journey has been designed to help you trace that same thread of divine love through every part of life. Through who you are, who you love, and who loves you. Month one reminded you that you can't give what you don't have. To love your neighbor well, you must first love yourself as God intended. Month two stretched you outward, challenging you to love people courageously and unconditionally. To love others the way Jesus loves you. Month three lifted your eyes upward, calling you to fall in love with God all over again through worship, obedience, and devotion. Lastly, month four brought you home, to the greatest truth of all. God loves you, perfectly, persistently, and permanently!

Together, these months form the rhythm of the Christian life. Every chapter of faith beats to the same divine drum: Love God. Love yourself. Love others. This is not just our Core Value. It's our calling. It is what Jesus declared as the greatest commandment, and it's the proof that we belong to Him.

As you close this book, I pray that you don't close its message. Let the love you've read about become the life you live out. Carry it into your family, your friendships, your workplace, your worship. Let it influence how you forgive, how you serve, and how you see yourself.

The world is watching! What it needs to see is love in motion. Not the shallow kind the culture sells, but the saving kind the cross supplied. When believers begin to love boldly, the Church becomes unstoppable. When we embody the Great Commandment, we fulfill the Great Commission.

So, live like you know that love wins. Because it always has, and it always will.

It won at the tomb. It wins in your testimony. And every time you choose grace over grudges, faith over fear, compassion over comfort, love wins again!

This is the heartbeat of Antioch Missionary Baptist Church.

This is the lifestyle of every disciple.

This is the anthem of the Kingdom.

Love wins forever and always.

Appendix

Antioch Missionary Baptist Church is a Christ-centered, Biblically based, Spiritually-led church that meets the needs of the total person by: Exalting the Savior, Evangelizing the Sinner, Equipping the Saved, Edifying the Saints and Encouraging every soul, through administrative Excellence by the power of the Holy spirit in Christ Jesus our Lord.

Our Core Values

1. Core Value 1 | The Great Commission

   We believe that the true mission of the church of God on earth is imbedded in the Great Commission Jesus gave His Disciples before departing the earth where He commanded that they *"Go ye therefore, and teach all nations, baptizing them in the name of the Father, and of the Son, and of the Holy Ghost: Teaching them to observe all things whatsoever I have commanded you: and, lo, I am with you alway, even unto the end of the world. Amen." (Matthew 28:19–20, KJV)*

2. Core Value 2 | The Great Commandment

   We believe that love is not optional it is essential. We are called to love God, love one another, and love ourselves according to the words of Jesus Christ. In this stead, we find the true trademark of every believer. Jesus put it on this wise, *"By this shall all men know that ye are my disciples, if ye have love one to another." (John 13:35, KJV)*

3. Core Value 3 — The Great Calling

   We are commanded to become fishers' of men. To reach them in the woeful seas of sin and to let them know that the Captain of the sea has heard their despairing cry and from the waters His grace will lift them and change their lives forever. Jesus gave this command to all who would dare follow Him when He said, *"Follow me, and I will make you fishers' of men." (St. Matthew 4:19, KJV)*

Together, these values define who we are at Antioch: a Christ-centered, Bible-based, Spirit-led church that meets the needs of the whole person.

Our Church Purpose Statement

To provide the Golden Triangle with an inclusive Christocentric ministry that effectively meets the needs of the total person: presenting the Gospel of our Lord Jesus Christ in a clear, contemporary, contextualized manner to all, so that persons might encounter the love of God is such a way that it would cause providential purpose to be revealed, pertinent potential to be released, and divine power to be received; changing the lives of people who will ultimately change the world.

FINAL WORD

"And now abideth faith, hope, love, these three; but the greatest of these is love."

(1 Corinthians 13:13, KJV)

Every page you've read, every prayer you've prayed, and every verse you've studied has been pointing toward this truth: Love is not just what God does—it's who He is.

And because He lives in you, Love Wins!

Other Books and Articles by John R. Adolph

I'm Changing the Game

Not Without A Fight

I'm Coming Out of This

Just Stick to the Script

Victorious Christian Living Volume I

Victorious Christian Living Volume II

Let Me Encourage You Volume I

Let Me Encourage You Volume II

The Him Book I

The Him Book II | The Anthology

Get Ready For Battle

Marriage Is For Losers

Celibacy Is For Fools

I Want Some Too

Victory: Ten FundAmen.tal Beliefs That Eradicate Defeat in the Life of a

Christian

Better Together

Based On A True Story

Back To The Table

Help Me Handle This

Necessary Changes

Articles-Zondervan Press

He Loves Me, He Loves Me, He Loves Me

I'm Certain That He Loves Me

His Love Made The Difference

God's Mind Is Made Up, He Loves You

Antioch Missionary Baptist Church
3920 W. Cardinal Drive Beaumont, TX 77705
Dr. John R. Adolph, Pastor
Website www.antiochbmt.org
FaceBook: Antioch Missionary Baptist Church
IG: @antiochbmt

Worship Service
Every Sunday at 8:00 am & 10:00 am
Virtual and Personal
Website: www.antiochbmt.org
YouTube: John R. Adolph Ministries LLC.

War Room Prayer Call
Every Wednesday at 7:00 am
YouTube: John R. Adolph Ministries LLC.

Bible Study
Every Thursday at 6:00 pm
Virtual and Personal
Website: www.antiochbmt.org
YouTube: John R. Adolph Ministries LLC.

John R. Adolph Ministries LLC.
The Message. The Ministry. The Man.
Website: www.jradolph.com
YouTube: John R. Adolph Ministries LLC.
FaceBook: John R. Adolph Ministries LLC.
IG: @iamjradolph

To purchase additional copies of this book or other books by Dr Adolph
or visit Amazon.com our bookstore website at:
www.advbookstore.com

Orlando, Florida, USA
"we bring dreams to life"™
www.advbookstore.com

Made in the USA
Coppell, TX
19 January 2026

69485897R00108